Three Keys to SPIRITUAL RENEWAL

Three Keys to SPIRITUAL RENEWAL

CLARK H. PINNOCK

BETHANY HOUSE PUBLISHERS
MINNEAPOLIS, MINNESOTA 55438
A Division of Bethany Fellowship, Inc.

Bible text in this publication is from the Revised Standard Version of the Bible, copyrighted 1946, 1952 © 1971, 1973 by the Division of Christian Education of the National Council of Churches of Christ in the USA, and used by permission.

Originally titled *The Untapped Power of Sheer Christianity* and published in Canada by the Welch Publishing Company, Inc.

Published by Bethany House Publishers
A Division of Bethany Fellowship, Inc.
6820 Auto Club Road, Minneapolis, Minnesota 55438

Printed in the United States of America

Library of Congress Cataloging-in-Publication Data

Pinnock, Clark H., 1937-
Three keys to spiritual renewal.

1. Spiritual life. 2. Church renewal. I. Title.
BV4501.2.P5543 1985 269 86-9645
ISBN 0-87123-6-656-7

This book is dedicated to

all the men and women who struggle for reformation and renewal in the churches of our land

and in loving memory of Francis A. Schaeffer who was valiant for the truth throughout a long and fruitful life

Other Books by Clark H. Pinnock

A Defense of Biblical Infallibility (1967)
Set Forth Your Case (1967)
A New Reformation: A Challenge to Southern Baptists (1968)
Evangelism and Truth (1969)
Biblical Revelation: Foundation of Christian Theology (1971)
Truth on Fire: The Message of Galatians (1972)
Toward a Theology for the Future (with David F. Wells, 1971)
Grace Unlimited (editor, 1975)
Reason Enough (1980)
The Scripture Principle (1985)

CONTENTS

INTRODUCTION
Three Keys to Renewal

I originally wrote this book under the strong conviction that we need a reformation and a renewal in the churches of Canada. But I believe the principles found here apply to the American church as well. We face a serious departure from biblical and evangelical truth which obscures our identity as God's people and hinders a clear message getting out to those who are lost.

A spirit of lethargy and deadness characterizes many of our congregations and prevents them from rejoicing in the Lord and getting the job done God gave us to do.

Although we are many in statistical terms, our impact upon society is minimal. We sit watching the country slide into more and more unrighteousness and secularism.

It makes me feel like Nehemiah when he heard about the desperate condition of Jerusalem: "(he) sat down and wept, and mourned for days" (1:4).

I ask myself, how can we evangelicals be so numerous and have so little impact upon our culture? How is it that we are nominal and tepid in our commitment to our great God? How can we treat his Word so casually and give God so little respect? When will the churches of Christ come to life and claim our nation for God? When will the sleeping giant rise?

I believe that we can have a reformation and renewal if we want it. God surely cannot be pleased with this situation of lukewarmness and ineffectiveness. But if we want to be revitalized, we must attend to *three important matters*, which forms the substance of this book. Let us begin by taking brief note of what these keys to renewal are.

The first key concerns our *identity*. Our theology and our preaching must be biblically sound. As a teacher of Christian theology, I am deeply burdened by the fact that there has been in the past century a tragic defection from the truth content of the Word of God. On every hand, in pulpits and seminary classrooms, plain scriptural truths which have been confessed and believed by Christians for two millennia are being set aside and subjected to withering criticism and outright denial. There is a spirit of revisionism at work in contemporary theology which aims to pervert the basic categories of the Christian proclamation and substitute another gospel for them. In fact, it is no gospel at all, because it points people to the inherent capacities of human beings for salvation rather than to the supernatural salvation of God in Christ. Unless we are good stewards of God's Word and return to the essentials of our biblical and apostolic faith, we cannot expect any blessing from God, but only wrath and judgment. There is a battle to be waged on behalf of gospel truth today. We must take a stand.[1]

The second key pertains to *vitality*. There is simply no way for the church to behave like the church if it suffers from spiritual lethargy. Unless we are filled with God's Spirit, we will not be inclined to praise God, spread the gospel, or obey God's commandments. Being Christian requires, and has always required, miracles of the Spirit. It never was intended that we should carry on the mission in our strength. We need the fresh touch and anointing of God upon us if we hope to break out of our current mediocrity. It is not enough to be biblically sound if we are not spiritually alive at the same time. There is not much to choose between a liberal and an orthodox church if they are both spiritually dead. We need God's presence and power to break through to revive and renew the church. We have to stop being so afraid of appearing to be pentecostal, and begin to look seriously at the spiritual graveyard which characterizes so many of our churches. I believe that God wants us to be radically open to him, and will start to bless us when we become willing. Then watch the sparks fly!

The third key relates to our *mission*. The whole point of God giving us his Word and his Spirit is in order for us to live out the gospel in the world and carry out the mission to the nations. We have been called to hold forth the Word of life and to shine as lights in the world, God wants the nations to be baptized, and to come under his teaching and discipline. Therefore, we have to take seriously the call to world evangelization and reclamation. Obviously I do not mean sanctifying worldly revolutions or substituting secular norms for the commands of God as is the habit of some today. What is required is that we take our global mission seriously and stop playing at it. God makes sovereign demands and claims upon all areas of creaturely life, not only on the private spiritual realm. Our world belongs to

God; it is our responsibility to claim it for him. We cannot expect God to bless us as long as we sit on our hands and refuse to get to work.

So there you have it. God is calling us to a more faithful *believing* of his Word, to a more profound *experiencing* of the Spirit, and to a more serious *practising* of our discipleship. We need to be sound in biblical doctrine, alive in our relationship with God, and serious in carrying out the mission God has given us. If we refuse to respond in these areas, I do not think we should expect much by way of the blessing and power of God to be upon us in the future.

But if we do get our message straight, and our religion vital, and our obedience worthy of the gospel, then we can get ready for the heavens to open and blessings to come which there will not be room enough to receive.

I write this book as a Christian theologian. This simply means that I belong to the pastoral leadership team which is charged with giving good counsel to the churches. Theology gives us access to the memory bank of the community, and makes it possible to discover old forgotten keys which can unlock some of our stubborn rusty locks today. Theology exists to jog the church's memory of truths it is in danger of forgetting but is in need of recalling because they can serve her well in the church's life and mission in our contemporary society.

More specifically I write as an evangelical theologian. This means that my insights come from the perspective of one who stands within the stream of historic Christianity, and confesses the great truths of incarnation and atonement, of salvation by grace through faith, and of our everlasting hope only in Jesus Christ. I am committed to the infallibility of the Bible as the norm and canon for our message, and stand staunchly against the modern revolt against all these truths.[2]

Finally I am not writing theoretically or abstractly. I feel keenly about my subject matter here. As a theologian I work where the battle for gospel truth rages fiercely. As a church member and deacon, I long for the church to come alive unto God. And as a Canadian citizen I grieve over the decline of North America into the secularist abyss and thirst for its Christian reconstruction.[3]

Now it is time to examine these three keys in more detail and to see how important each is in the renewal we pray and work for in North America.

1

THE FIRST KEY:

"Loving the Truth"

Before speaking about the great defection in Christian theology from the sound basis of God's inspired Word, let me describe how things stood before this sad departure took place.

Faithful Stewards

A Christian is a person according to the New Testament who believes, receives, and loves the truth. Formerly slaves of sin, believers "have become obedient from the heart to the standard of teaching to which they were committed" (Rom 6:17). They have received the truth about Jesus Christ, and now seek to be rooted and built up in him (Col 2:6-7). In contrast with those who refuse to love the truth and be saved, the Christian loves it and receives it (2 Thess 2:10). He or she is a student enrolled in the school of Christ, learning from him and about him (Eph 4:20-21). We are incorporated as believers into a holy temple which is established upon the foundations laid by the apostles and prophets (Eph 2:20). Far from faith being merely intellectual assent to doctrinal propositions, getting to know the truth is like drinking spiritual milk and eating nourishing food (1 Pet 2:1,1 Tim 4:6).

For this reason, the New Testament warns us about false teaching. We are not supposed to be like children swayed by every wind of doctrine but full of faith and understanding (Eph 4:14). Paul expresses his own fear lest young believers be seduced by Satan's cunning, and have their thoughts led astray from a sincere and pure devotion to Christ (2 Cor 11:2). Even though there is no other gospel than the good news of Christ, there are counterfeit versions of it circulating which must be challenged and soundly refuted (Gal 1:6-9).

As if to underline the fact that being a Christian involves believing and loving the truth of the gospel, the New Testament also warns us about false teachers and urges us to ordain only sound teachers. In a striking prophecy, so abundantly fulfilled in our own time, Paul writes: "For the time is coming when people will not endure sound teaching, but having itching ears they will accumulate for themselves teachers to suit their own likings, and will turn away from listening to the truth and wander into myths" (2 Tim 4:3-4). Peter also warns us about false teachers who will bring in destructive heresies, even denying the Master who bought them (2 Pet 2:1). As we shall see, such warnings are an accurate description of what has actually happened in modern theology.

True ministers of the gospel, on the other hand, are to be faithful stewards of God's mysteries (1 Cor 4:1-2). As Paul put it: "We have renounced disgraceful, underhanded ways; we refuse to practise cunning or to tamper with God's Word, but by the open statement of the truth we would commend ourselves to every man's conscience in the sight of God" (2 Cor 4:2). We did not invent our message out of our own experience or imagination. We have no right to tamper with it, to add or subtract from it. We gladly submit to the message God gave us in his Word, and refuse to subject it to our reasoning. Our task is to preach God's Word, in season and out of season (2 Tim 4:2). We are heralds of a glorious message about what God has done to save sinners, and we must not shrink from declaring the whole counsel of God (Acts 20:27).

Because it is so important that this message of salvation be preached with integrity and content, we are commanded to guard the gospel (2 Tim 1:14) and to ensure that it is passed along to other faithful teachers who will continue to proclaim it (2 Tim 2:2). Paul tells us what a Christian minister must be: "he must hold firm to the sure word as taught, so that he may be able to give instruction in sound doctrine and also to confute those who contradict it" (Titus 1:9). Where the gospel is being denied, it is essential to do what Jude says: "to contend for the faith which was once for all delivered to the saints" (Jude 3). What a travesty it is when church theologians and leaders today, not only do not hold fast to the gospel, but actually openly criticize and revise it.

Enough New Testament texts have been cited to prove that being a Christian is not merely an experience or a lifestyle — it involves believing and loving the truth of the gospel message. This message is not merely a product of the human imagination but an expression of the mind of God. We are not talking here about some kind of scholastic concern to be precise in every last jot and tittle of our message, but rather about faithfulness to the gospel of salvation through Jesus Christ given to us through the apostles. Of this precious truth deposit, the church is the pillar and the bulwark (1 Tim 3:15).[1]

It was this belief, namely that God had vouchsafed a definitive message to the church in the beginning, which prompted Christians to treasure the teachings and writings of the apostles. The setting aside of the New Testament as the foundation for the church's ministry and message was not an official action of the bishops in council. It was more like an instinctive recognition of God's authority resident in these books. Even in the New Testament itself we find Peter referring to the letters of Paul as if on a par with the Old Testament scriptures (2 Peter 3:16). And in the earliest writings such as the Didache, Ignatius, and Barnabas we find that the New Testament literature, particularly the gospels and the epistles, was being used in an authoritative way as the scriptures of the church. It was the natural continuation of what Luke describes in Acts: "they (the early Christians) devoted themselves to the apostles' teaching and fellowship, to the breaking of bread and the prayers" (2:42). From the beginning the authority of the apostles was recognized, an authority which first attached to their oral teaching, and then to their writings as well.

This is what was meant by the Council of Constantinople in 381 AD when it spoke of the church as 'apostolic'. The church was founded upon the teachings of the apostles and the Lord. Faithfulness to this standard is one of the marks of the true church. It has been gathered by the original preaching of the apostles and is united by their witness to Christ later embodied in their writings. If the church is true to her calling, it will walk in glad continuity with the apostles. He who does not hear the apostles does not hear the Lord, who is known through their basic witness. This witness is for all subsequent time the norm of our Christian existence in preaching and in living. The church must ever be confronted with this message and taught to believe and confess it.

The form in which the message of the apostles comes to us is in the writings of the New Testament, based upon the scriptures of the Hebrews. These writings have from the first been recognized and approved by the communities of Christians as the apostolic norm. The New Testament canon is therefore the means by which the church discerns the spirits and distinguishes true from false teaching. An authentic congregation is one which is soundly based in this original apostolic testimony to Jesus Christ.[2]

What the apostolic canon is concerned with is of course the gospel message. By having such a norm and standard, the church is in a position to say what the good news is. It is able confidently to confess her faith in Christ the Lord of the universe and Saviour of the world, in accord with the New Testament original message. God's kingdom has come nigh (Mark 1:15). A Saviour has been born (Matthew 1:23 Luke 2:11). God has sent his own Son into the world (John 3:16). By shedding his blood, the Lord Jesus has saved us from the wrath of God, and reconciled us to the Father (Romans 3:25 5:1, 6-11). God was in Christ, reconciling the world to himself, not imputing our sins to us, but rather laying them upon Christ (2 Cor 5:19-21). He became a curse for us, delivering us from this present evil age, and bestowing upon us the status of adoption (Gal 1:4 3:13 4:4-7). God has chosen us — Christ has redeemed us — the Spirit has sealed us (Eph 1:3-14). We are alive in him, and joined to the new people of God (Eph 2:1-22). Hallelujah!

By identifying the New Testament as canon and authority, the early church guaranteed, not that every point would always be clear and undisputed (obviously this has not happened), but the basic categorial structure of the Christian message would be fixed for all ages. It means that Christians will always want to speak of a sovereign God, of the holy trinity, of the divine-human Saviour, of the outpoured Holy Spirit, of the substitutionary atonement on the cross, of the bodily resurrection and visible return of Jesus Christ. It is this glorious message of salvation through Christ which we guard and proclaim. What characterizes historic Christianity, and distinguishes it so sharply from modern theology, is its sturdy backbone of solid truth to which it pledges itself. Against the disintegration of this structure we must stand on guard today.[3]

To avoid misinterpretation, I do not mean that we have done our duty when we have repeated the biblical message and made no effort to relate it effectively to the contemporary audience. Theology is like an ellipse with two foci. It is important both to take account of the Word of God and also to communicate it meaningfully to modern persons. We are obliged to be both conservative (faithful to the truth deposit) and contemporary (creative in communicating the truth in fresh ways). To spell that out a little more, I have added an appendix to this book.

The Great Defection

The reader would be greatly mistaken if he thought that the style and content of theology I have been discussing up to now were universally held by contemporary Christians. In actual fact we face a full-scale revolt against Christianity as it has been historically understood and a new form of religion which is very different. Let me try to explain how this state of affairs came about.

The blame has to be laid, in my opinion, at the door of the secularist Enlightenment. In the 18th century in Europe there arose a philosophy and way of thinking which had no place for God. Some people blame it on the rise of science, but this does not seem fair. Science itself has deeply Christian roots, and most of the great scientists prior to the 20th century at least were staunch Christians — many still are. It is not science, but scientism which is to blame, a spirit of godlessness which has pervaded Western thinking. People have come to believe in their own unlimited goodness and power. They have decided that they can get along perfectly well without God, for God is not a hypothesis they feel they need.

In order to create space for this new religion of Promethean man, it was necessary to deal some death blows to historic Christianity. This was attempted in the work of Hume and then Kant who set out to destroy the intellectual foundations of the gospel and make it impossible for Christians to challenge successfully the new secularism. So these exceedingly able philosophers chipped away at the basis of Christian apologetics, dogmatics, and ethics until there was nothing left to stand on in their opinion. In a pleasant gesture they offered to let religion continue so long as it promised not to make any truth claims uncongenial to godless thinking. They would graciously allow religion to exist 'within the bounds of reason'. But let no theologian dare to suggest that he had any rational basis for the orthodox faith.

Thus, in the wake of a savage critique, a bargain was struck: if theologians agreed to revise what they meant by Christianity and placed it in a kind of upper story or existential realm where it would not bother the secularists, peace could be enjoyed. Understandably, some theologians were aghast at the suggestion, while others were inclined to take up the offer.

Contemporary theology, in my view, is divided along two lines indicated by this secularist challenge. First, we have the classical Christians who like good Tareyton smokers would rather fight than switch and second, the liberals, who elected to accommodate theology to secularism in the hopes of saving some of the truth. Thus we have a theology with a radically new face, a theology which is prepared to revise Christianity very considerably in order to stay in the good graces of modern reason. The most important fact about modern theology is the split between what we might call the theology of resistance and the theology of accommodation. These represent the two obvious responses one could make to the secularist assault. One affirms the truth of God's infallible Word, while the other is based on human experience and hence operates out of subjectivity. No difference between historic traditions (i.e., Catholic and Protestant) is nearly as great as the difference that exists between these two theological approaches. Machen was not exaggerating when he spoke of Christianity and liberalism, for it is difficult to describe the new theology by the old name.

All this is very real to me from my own life experience. I was brought up in a social church where the gospel was not clearly explained or confidently confessed. Fortunately I came under the influence of a godly grandmother who lived with us during her declining years and a Sunday School teacher who loved the Word of God. Both of them were greatly dissatisfied with the diluted Christianity in my home congregation. But they led me to the Lord, and instilled in me a powerful love for God and a deep confidence in the Bible. We prayed and sang together, and the Spirit bore witness with my spirit to the truth of the gospel. But I remember feeling appalled at the omission of the central gospel themes both in my church and in other churches like it. I could not understand (and still cannot) why certain preachers and their people did not delight in the orthodox gospel of the Word of God. It has been about thirty years since I was saved, and I have never been able to shake off the feeling of outrage at the arrogance of the liberal decision to revise the New Testament message to make it acceptable to modern men. I suppose that my deepest concern as a theologian today is to expose and refute this deadly error.[4]

What is liberal theology? It is essentially a salvage operation, designed to rescue whatever can be saved, after secularism has been allowed to do its thing. It asks, what can we believe now that historic Christianity has been wasted by the acids of secularist criticism? Liberal theology is an orderly retreat from the biblical faith. It gives historic Christianity a decent burial. In order to avoid a direct clash with secularism, the liberals engaged in some crucial cognitive bargaining and agreed to shift to altogether new ground.

First, they agreed not to defend the biblical faith as if it were an objective claim. For example, they agreed not to defend belief in God as a fully rational belief or belief in the resurrection of Jesus as a historical fact. Godless scepticism would not take kindly to these efforts. Instead, most of the liberals decided to relocate the burden of Christianity in the realm of experience. Having lost their intellectual nerve, they decided to retreat inward. Henceforth faith would be thought of as an expression of spirituality rather than conveying universally valid truth. In this way they placed religion in a nice safe haven where the critics would not be able to bother it. Although this was certainly true, not all of the liberals read the price tag on this retreat: the unbeliever would never again have to take the gospel seriously as an objective truth claim.

Second, and this is even more serious, the liberals backed away from the historic Christian confidence in the truth of the biblical testimony. They decided not to see it as a revealed message given by God, but as a set of merely human symbols arising out of human experience. As Langdon Gilkey put it:

> Under the impact of the growth of physical science, (religious liberalism) changed the conception of Christian truth from that of divinely given and so infallible propositions about all manner of things in heaven, on earth, and in history . . . into a system of human, and so relative, symbols which elucidate the depth and mystery of existence but do not compete directly with either scientific or historical knowledge . . . it changed the understanding of Christian doctrine from that of eternal statements of unchanging and thus unalterable validity, to that of relative human statements of Christian truth for their time, statements that reflect their own cultural situation and needs.[5]

No longer then would it be necessary for a theologian to affirm any of the biblical themes just because they were original, unless it happened to agree with what he was already feeling. This is of course a plain denial of the apostolicity of the church, and if unresisted would spell the death of Christianity as we have understood it.

The Christian message has all of a sudden become, according to religious liberalism, not the glorious revealed gospel of Jesus Christ, but a set of humanly derived existential symbols, which may do something for the believer, but certainly do not need to be announced to the world as if God had given them. Faithfulness to the gospel now no longer means holding firmly to the truths of saving revelation, but something vague like agreeing with the spirit of Jesus and his community over time. No wonder it is impossible to define the 'message' of religious liberalism. Beliefs arise from human experience, and therefore none of them are normative beyond that experience. Liberal 'Christianity' has no clear identity at all and cannot say who a Christian is. In the guise of being 'honest to God' a person can deny almost every tenet of the Christian faith and substitute another gospel in their place and there is no way to call him to account. For Christianity is no longer thought to involve objective and verifiable truth and can be made to order at the behest of subjective feelings. No wonder theology today is in the chaotic and open-ended state it is. (It would be even more chaotic were it not for the fact that liberal theologians usually inhabit traditional churches which require them to make some affirmations of faith they would probably have lost were they outside them. The flip side of course is the harm and confusion these theologians create in those churches where they really do not belong.)

We face a great defection today. Liberal theology has abandoned the biblical message in its cognitive dimensions, and transformed Christianity into something very different from that which Calvin, Wesley and the great evangelical tradition preached and believed. The gospel is being betrayed before our very eyes.[6]

But, it will be asked, is it fair to depict what has undoubtedly happened after the manner of a defection with overtones of betrayal? Could it not better be seen as a struggle between two ways of knowing: the traditional way which views the gospel as a message coming from God, untouched by human history and culture, and the liberal or modern way which sees it as historically and humanly conditioned and not an absolute claim? Yes indeed we could see it that way, and say that this shift in epistemology lies beneath the shift from content to experience. Does that make it any better? Is it still not a decision to refuse the gospel on its own terms as a God-given deposit, in order to view it in terms acceptable to us? If the gospel is not the everlasting gospel of the Lord, would it not be better to leave it alone, and stop trying to pretend that we can affirm it while actually denying it? Of course epistemic assumptions lie beneath the conflict between the classical and the liberal believer, but we must say that the liberal historicist assumptions are in contradiction with the truth claim of the Word of God and therefore unacceptable. One is free to decide that historicism is true, namely that it is impossible to believe in a universally valid message from God which cannot be accounted for in merely human and cultural terms. But having decided thus, one is not free afterwards to go on professing to be Christian, and twisting the gospel into something very different from what it is.[7]

So what we have here in modern theology is a major shift concerning what the gospel is and what the criteria are for deciding. Once we move away from the Bible as the infallible norm to human experience as a basis for divine truth, then one need not be very bright to predict what will happen next. Obviously not one single detail in the Christian system of truth is likely to remain the same, unless for reasons of nostalgia. This is indeed the case, as anyone who is reasonably literate in matters theological knows. We are faced with a wholesale revision of classical theology on the basis of completely new foundations. In order to appreciate the extent of the change which has occurred, let us explore the ways in which some of the topics of systematic theology have been handled by liberals.

Counterfeit Christianity

First, the doctrine of revelation and our knowledge of God is completely turned around. In the past, the reader will recall, people believed that God had revealed his character and will both in the creation and in salvation history, making it possible for humans to know him in a saving way through Jesus Christ. Two important changes have now been introduced in liberal theology. First, what we call general revelation has been blown out of all proportion and transformed into the possibility of salvation. Almost to a man, the liberals now say that God can be savingly encountered in the depths of the human heart and that Christians do not need to trouble people of other religions with imperialistic claims about Jesus being the only way. Why preach the gospel to every creature when it is perfectly possible for them to encounter God in the context of their religion and culture? Why trouble them with the demand that they be converted to Christ and be baptized? Needless to say this opinion spells the end of missionary work in the traditional sense. Social and political action have rushed in to replace it.[8]

Second, the Bible is no longer considered to be the written Word of God, but something much less. Its content is no longer regarded to be authoritative because it is the work of the human imagination. The function of the Bible is not to convey infallible information now, but to serve as a vehicle of existential experience. These human symbols have the power to evoke in the hearer and reader a human liberation of some kind. The authority of scripture does not reside in its content, but in its power to occasion experiences of revelation in us, and leaves us free to conceptualize what is meant as best we may. This leaves theology with no guidelines and completely open-ended. This is of course a flat denial of the Bible as the canon of the church. But, one might ask, could it not be seen in less drastic terms, as a change in what the function of the Bible is? Yes, certainly it can. But it is a change from what the authority of the Bible claims to possess (and the churches have always recognized it to possess) to viewing it in existential terms, thus removing the entire foundation of revealed truth from Christian theology. Like so much in liberal theology, the moves can be made to sound harmless and even beneficial, until suddenly it dawns upon us that a revolution has taken place. If the Bible is merely a human witness, if it can be limitlessly critiqued, if it derives from the mind of man in a fundamental way, then we have no certain message or hope. The Reformation which called the church back to the written Word of God has been reversed and overthrown, and we have a crisis in theology the likes of which we have never seen before. Heresies there have always been, on this topic or that. But a heresy that questions the very foundations of our knowing God and salvation is uniquely threatening and monstrous from a Christian point of view. It attacks the very foundations of the gospel, and leaves us nothing to hang on to.[9]

It may be that some conservatives are barking up the wrong tree when they determine to fight the battle for the Bible around the category of inerrancy. But nuances aside, there can be no doubt that there is a crisis of the scripture principle, and that all classical Christians have a basic stake in it. Nothing less than the primacy of Scripture for theology is up for grabs in the modern discussion.[10]

Third, one of the prime targets of sceptical philosophy in modern times has been belief in God. It has been argued that belief in God is not a rational belief, and that knowledge about God is denied to finite minds. Human categories cannot be applied to One who transcends the universe. There is a thick wall separating God and ourselves which cannot be penetrated. Therefore, religion must now content itself with human feelings of God, and not make any cognitive claims about God. This gives rise to different errors, either thinking of God as infinitely transcending the world and forever unknowable, or as filling the world immanentally and showing up anonymously in the depths of existence. Or, if it is decided that belief in God is not any longer meaningful to modern man, it is always possible to speak of a 'gospel of Christian atheism' as Thomas Altizer does. Although death of God theology generally evokes a chuckle from liberal and conservative alike, it should not, because it is merely a logical working out of liberal presuppositions going right back to Schleiermacher. The shift from the objective Word of God in Scripture to the subjective religious feelings of mankind has no logical stopping place; it threatens to obliterate every single Christian belief. Most liberals of course believe in God, but what is unclear is why they do so and what they mean by God. At least with the radicals, you know where they stand and why.

My point is simply that the defection we are speaking of affects the doctrine of God as well as other topics, and means that one can no longer speak with any confidence about the sovereign God who reveals himself and gives us his Word in human language. And that means one cannot speak with confidence about the good news.[11]

Fourth, the cluster of doctrines where most Christians will instantly notice the shift encompasses the person and the work of Christ and their bearing upon salvation. "For no other foundation can any one lay than that which is laid, which is Christ Jesus" (1 Cor 3:11). Nevertheless, the foundation is being eroded on every side today.

To begin with, although no one denies the true humanity of Jesus, few theologians would want to follow Thomas and confess of him — "My Lord and my God" (John 20:28). We now hear talk of 'the myth of God incarnate', as if belief in the incarnation were only a Christian way of mapping religious experience and not the supreme miracle and eucatastrophe (Tolkien's term) by which God has reconciled the world. The modern way of denying the deity of Christ is to appear to affirm it without actually doing so. Gilkey for example will speak of the Christ-event which constitutes for him a unique disclosure of the grace and love of God. Jesus is only human like each of us except that he embodies spiritually and morally what God intends for us all to be and provides a window into ultimate reality.[12]

Everywhere we confront a revelation-Christology which says many true things except the all-important truth that God the Son entered into history in Jesus of Nazareth to accomplish a supernatural redemption. It must be said definitively and dogmatically that if Jesus is no more than ideal and normative man, a revelation of the love of God, then he cannot save us in the way the New Testament proclaims he did save us. An ideal man, however special and unique, cannot become the Saviour of a ruined race. He simply is not 'big' enough. The most important way in which Jesus is unique is precisely in his being God incarnate. His eternal deity underlies his uniqueness as man and the efficacy of his atoning work.[13] Jesus is not only an example for our faith, he is the object of our faith.

The meaning of the cross of Christ too has suffered a terrible decline in modern theology. At the very heart of the evangel is the proclamation that Christ died for our sins. Not his life but his death saves us. Not the incarnation alone but what took place on Calvary brings us grace and forgiveness. Christ died in our place. He became a curse for us. A propitiation has been made to take away the guilt of sin and wash away the pollution of our sins. Bearing our griefs and sorrows, Jesus offered up his life as a ransom for many. Therefore, and on that basis alone, we have been justified by faith.

Yet despite all the evidence of the Bible and the massiveness of the tradition on this point, you will look long to find a really modern theologian who forthrightly affirms the vicarious substitution of Jesus Christ on the cross. We are told that God does not need to be propitiated, that sins can be pardoned without the shedding of blood. It is said that Jesus was God's representative rather than man's substitute. We are told that the purpose of his death was its transforming impact upon our hardened hearts. In short, all manner of half-truths are provided, while practically a total silence exists upon the main thing: . . . "he has appeared once for all at the end of the age to put away sin by the sacrifice of himself" (Hebrews 9:26). As Paul says, . . . "God was in Christ reconciling the world to himself, not counting their trespasses against them . . ." (2 Cor 5:19). "For our sake he (God) made him (Christ) to be sin who knew no sin, so that in him we might become the righteousness of God" (2 Cor 5:21).

Let me be perfectly plain. The only basis on which you and I have any hope of standing in the presence of God justified is the shed blood of Jesus Christ. In obscuring this truth, modern theology is guilty of the worst possible crime against the gospel. Indeed the whole dismal picture here reminds one of the warning issued in the New Testament in response to a similar problem: "How much worse punishment do you think will be deserved by the man who has spurned the Son of God, and profaned the blood of the covenant by which he was sanctified, and outrages the Spirit of grace?" (Hebrews 10:29)[14]

Similarly with respect to the resurrection of Christ we see the same kind of backing away from what the New Testament proclaims. Whereas in the Bible this event is the miracle in which God vindicates the claims of Christ and seals his atoning work by powerfully endorsing it, modern theologians are busy trying to reinterpret it and in the process deny it. Many of them follow Bultmann and label the resurrection mythical thinking, incredible to modern man (they mean, to themselves). The 'resurrection' then becomes the experience of new life which the disciples received and not a bothersome miracle at all. Kaufman goes so far as to suggest that God gave them an hallucination to make them believe in resurrection. But whatever the shifty move, a terrific effort is being made to deny that Jesus' tomb was empty on the third day. Why? Because modern unbelief, calling itself scientific, has declared such miracles to be impossible, and the theologians, who are always eager to please the secularists, have agreed to make the resurrection unmiraculous. Thus Christianity, which for centuries was a religion of the glorious resurrection, has now been changed into something else. It is part of a godless move to edge God out of his creation and the logic is of course atheistic. God himself is by all accounts the most supernatural Fact there is, totally dwarfing a mere resurrection. The mystery to me has always been why people like Bultmann cannot see that what is really unacceptable to modern man is just God. Why play around with trivia like virgin birth and resurrection when the basis of those mighty acts is retained? Why in heaven's name does demythologizing stop short of God? The sad answer is that in the truly radical theologians it does not. It is just that most liberals lack the courage of their convictions, and refuse to follow the direction of their own logic to its ultimate end.[15]

The point of all this denial and revision is to change the meaning of salvation. Large numbers of people under the influence of humanism do not want to believe that man is guilty and lost and can be saved only by faith in the crucified and living Redeemer. Therefore, everything is being done to retune theology at every point where it bears upon this disagreeable soteriology. We have already mentioned some of them. It is now being said that salvation is within the reach of everyone within the context of their own culture and religion if any. God is everywhere graciously present, and it is not important to hear and respond to the gospel of Christ itself. Indeed, according to John Hick, Christ is the saviour myth of Christians, and not the Saviour of the world as the Bible says. Christ mediates God to people in Western culture, but God is mediated in a hundred ways in other cultures. It is not true that an atoning sacrifice was made on behalf of guilty sinners, and not important that all creatures learn of that fact. Any one can be saved simply by opening themselves to God in their place without ever having to put their trust in Christ. One of the most startling about-faces in the history of theology happened when the Roman Catholic church at Vatican Two, under the influence of liberal theology seeping in to its traditions through Karl Rahner, declared that Jews, Muslims, Hindus, and even atheists, so long as they are sincerely seeking truth, will be saved. There is no word about the importance of their being converted or born again or delivered from God's wrath. And if this is what is being said in the Catholic church, which is orthodox on all the points we have just discussed, what do you suppose is the attitude in those liberal Protestant circles where there is little soundness from head to foot?

Do not misunderstand me. I am a universalist myself in the biblical sense. God is engaged in reconciling the world. God so loved the whole world that he sent his Son to save it. I have no interest in a pseudo-gospel which leaves out most of the human race. But I have to ask how God will save the race. Is it not through the finished work of the Son of God? Have we not been commissioned in no uncertain terms to go and make disciples of all nations, baptizing them in the triune name? Are we not justified solely by faith in his blood? Is it not enough to know that the Judge of the whole earth will do right? (Genesis 18:25). And is it not enough to know that our responsibility is to summon people to call upon the name of the Lord Jesus? I predict, that if this kind of creeping universalism continues, the effect will be (it is already plain) that missionary interest will dry up altogether except among those biblical people who continue to believe the everlasting gospel.

To engage in this sorrowful litany of theological defections is a sad business. What is happening is nothing less than a remaking and unmaking of Christian doctrine.[16] Practically the entire categorical framework of the evangel is being picked apart and dismantled, not by every religious liberal in the same way and to the same degree. But it is in a cumulative way and the overall effect is the obliteration of the way of salvation. We ought to be ashamed at the fact that we evangelicals who are determined not to let this happen are so little shocked and outraged by it. Each publishing season we anticipate a new set of heresies and pin them up on the bulletin boards of contemporary theology. And we forget to weep at the outrage and the damage this is doing to the young ones who believe in God. We ought to remember these words of the Lord: "Whoever causes one of these little ones who believe in me to sin, it would be better for him to have a great millstone fastened round his neck and to be drowned in the depth of the sea" (Matthew 18:6).

What we have been describing as a great defection is quite easily explained. Liberal theology has decided to accommodate the gospel to the demands of secular modernity. It wants to bring Christian thinking close alongside humanist thinking so that it will be easy to make the transition from the one to the other. In effect liberal theology comes to secular humanism, hat in hand, offering to make radical concessions in order to obtain acceptance and a membership card to the modern world. In order to see this, all you have to do is to compare twentieth-century humanist thought with the metaphysical, moral, and political content of liberal theology. It turns out that they say practically the same things. Do we want freedom from dogma? control over our bodies? evolution in the schools? religion without real revelation? Christianity without cross or resurrection? moral relativism? the equality of all faiths? the celebration of human experiences and achievements? There is a whole set of humanist opinions today to which the liberal theologians have managed to accommodate 'Christianity'.

The irony of course is that the strategy has been a hopeless failure. If the idea was to convert modern man by making concessions to his philosophy and lifestyle, then there is little evidence of any success. Quite the contrary in fact. The great examples of conversions in the 20th century have been in the other direction. C.S. Lewis, T.S. Eliot, and Malcolm Muggeridge, for example, were converted to orthodox doctrine not to liberalism. And why is that? Because liberal theology is such thin soup, which offers nothing to nourish souls starved at secular tables. And it is even worse than that. Not only are the liberals not gaining converts, they are rapidly losing the followers they once had. Why remain in a liberal church if the message is hardly distinguishable from the humanistic culture outside it? Either find a faithful church, or drop out altogether. Liberal theology is not an entrance into the church for modern men — it is an exit from the church for people who have lost faith. The liberal church is essentially the agent of secularization within the religious community. The real humanists know this, and hence have no interest in this kind of 'Christianity'. They just take one look, and realize that their negative view of biblical religion has been accepted by the liberal theologians as well, so that it is only a matter of time until the liberals become plain humanists themselves.[17]

Fortunately the future of Christianity does not lie with the liberals. It would have no future if it did. The growth of Bible-believing communities is astonishing and unmistakable. There is, it turns out, a hunger for the real gospel. The revival of true religion against all predictions two decades ago is enough to make one believe in God. As a theologian I am especially gratified to see colleagues coming back to biblical faith after years of wandering in liberal wastelands. I refer not only to new conservative voices like Royce Gruenler and Thomas Oden, but also to pastors like my friend Bill who accepted the liberal line at seminary and went out only to lose his faith altogether. But thanks be to God, after a period of soul-sorrow, he was restored to Jesus Christ through the ministry of healing in his child at the hands of Catholic charismatics. In response he flung himself again upon the mercy of God. Now he stands tall and true for the biblical faith, and ready to fulfil the ministry from which he was sidetracked so many years earlier. Joan Baez asks in song: "When will we ever learn?" Praise God — there are good signs we are learning now.

But how, given the great pluralism of contemporary theology, can one so simplify the situation so as to imply that there are really only two types of theology: classical theology based on scripture, and liberal theology based in human experience above all? The answer is, that there are various levels of analysis. On the superficial and obvious level there are a great variety of theologies — liberation, process, hope, play, kerygmatic, manifestation, secular, story theology and so on. *But at the deepest level there are only two.* Whether it be a theology of hope or a theology of story, the deep question to pose is this: does this theology take for its criterion the teachings of scripture or not? Does it consider itself bound by what the Bible says or not? Does it give God speaking in scripture the last word or not? After that decision is made of course theology may follow one line or another, but the decision itself will determine radically its direction. Although there may appear to be many types of theology, at the deepest level, in my opinion, there are only two, and we must choose between them whether we want to or not.[18]

Recovering The Essentials

If we hope for the blessing of God to rest upon our lives and our witness, we must get back to the essentials of the biblical and evangelical faith. We must cease the practice of tampering with God's Word, and in repentance begin to hold it fast. It was encouraging to see how Karl Barth turned from anthropocentric theology to theology based upon exegesis of the Holy Scriptures. It is good to hear fresh voices like Keith Ward's replying to the modernism of a Don Cupitt in his book *Holding Fast to God.* It gives us joy to find theologians like Donald Bloesch writing about *The Essentials of Evangelical Theology.* It is promising to see Royce Gruenler and others like him turning away from process theology and embracing the biblical faith again. In my own denomination it is encouraging to see a church which had strayed from its biblical roots beginning to regain its footing and to insist upon the importance of sound doctrine. We seem to be on the road to reformation in Canada although there is still a long way to travel. The church has been deeply compromised, and the healing will take a long time.

As we move toward reformation, it is important to recognize that the restoration of doctrinal soundness is not always achieved in the best possible way. For example, liberalism often creates a fundamentalist reaction to itself which does not think very deeply about the issues we all face, and does not interpret the Bible very profoundly. There is often the tendency to narrow down the truth to a few fundamental points, and even to include in them points of dubious value. If, for example, we make opinions about eschatology or baptism or apologetics into touchstones of orthodoxy, we divide true believers from one another and even pervert the gospel to a certain extent. Sometimes the problem can be a mean-spiritedness or an unwillingness to be fair to one's adversaries which spoils the effort to be true to God's Word. In our experience in Baptist circles in Ontario, for example, the point T.T. Shields was making about doctrinal laxity at McMaster University was heard only by a minority because of the way this great preacher handled the work of polemical criticism. He tended to exaggerate his case, making the struggle too much a clash of personalities, so that a denomination was split and the valid point he was making was discredited.

At an even deeper level it is possible that we can think ourselves faithful to the Bible when in fact we are guilty of twisting it to make it agree with our own philosophy or lifestyle. Conservatives too can accommodate the gospel and force it into line with the values of modernity. How many conservative Christians today seem to be actively involved in reaching the lost and in applying biblical values to contemporary society? Before we point a finger at the undoubted liberal accommodation, let us examine our own lives and behaviour and ask if we have not domesticated the Word of God as well?

There is a difference of course when we speak of conservative accommodation. These are people who believe the Word of God but are acting inconsistently with it, and therefore can be summoned back to obedient faith. With the liberal accommodation, because it involves a defection from scriptural authority, there is no basis to appeal to in calling for proper obedience and discipleship. There can hardly be a reformation if the instrument and criterion of reform has already been discarded. Thus any conservative accommodation is corrigible in principle, whereas liberal accommodation is not. Nevertheless, it is shocking when those who are seeking to be faithful to God's Word put stumbling blocks in the way of others and make it harder for them to see the wonderful light of the glory of God in the face of Jesus Christ.

As we move back to evangelical soundness, it may be good for us to confess our faith afresh. There are two opposite dangers here. A church can have a creed which it inherited from the past and merely recite it week by week. On the other hand, it can have no confession at all and exist in a doctrinal vacuum. What we need are statements of faith which articulate the biblical faith in fresh language and respond to the heresies which exist at the present moment. It is not usually enough to return to past confessions, which, although they provide guidelines for correct belief, do not carry the power and authority they once did for people. What we need are confessions soundly based in Scripture which also capture the urgency of the situation and ring with spiritual authenticity. The confession which follows was written by me in the context of the Baptist Renewal Fellowship of Canada in its search for a fresh, contemporary statement of faith.

A NEW BAPTIST CONFESSION

Believing in the essentials of the faith as taught in the Bible and expressed in the great ecumenical, Protestant, and evangelical confessions of earlier days, we gladly bear witness to the following articles which are crucial to our life, ministry, and mission as Baptists:

God has spoken

We rejoice that God has revealed himself and spoken savingly to us in the events and words of redemptive history recorded in Scripture. This history reached fulfilment in Jesus Christ, the Word of God incarnate, who makes himself known to us through the Spirit and by means of the Bible.

We believe that the Bible, as the Scripture of the churches, is an essential part and trustworthy record of the gracious divine self-disclosure. We believe that all the books of the Old and New Testaments, having been given by inspiration of God, are the written Word of God, the only infallible rule of faith and practice. Scripture is the criterion of our beliefs and we submit ourselves to the test of its teachings. The Bible is to be interpreted according to the original context and purpose and in reverent obedience to the Lord who speaks through it in living power. We wholeheartedly acknowledge the full authority of the Bible.

He is the living God

We joyfully acknowledge that God has revealed himself to us as the living and true God, perfect in love and righteous in all his ways. Being one in his eternal essence, God exists in three persons, Father, Son, and Spirit, so that we know him as the triune God. The Father we know to be the missionary God who sent forth His Son to be our saviour and sends His Spirit to be our companion. He therefore sends us out to make known his saving purpose among all nations. Being also the God who loves justice, he has promised to bring his kingdom to the world, and summon us to be witnesses to the kingdom.

The Son who came preaching the kingdom of God we confess to be fully divine and truly human in the oneness of his person. God the Son, the eternal Word, became flesh for the sake of our salvation and we confess him to be our divine and risen Lord.

The Spirit bears witness to the risen and exalted Lord and applies to us personally the blessings of the gospel. We look to the Spirit for the enrichment of our faith and for a fresh outpouring of power for our mission in the world.

He is creator, sustainer, and perfecter

We wish to give glory to God, from whom and through whom and to whom are all things. He is the creator of the whole universe visible and invisible. By His Word and for His glory the world was created out of nothing and made to be a habitation for us. For this reason we treasure, respect, and conserve the earth.

God is also Lord and King over all that he has made. In his power and wisdom he sustains, rules over, and cares for the universe and its inhabitants. He works all things together for good to those who love Him, and therefore we do not fear.

God is also the source of our hope, as the One who will perfect the world spoiled by sin and bring in his glorious kingdom. He has promised to make all things new so that we can live in joyous hope. We eagerly anticipate the visible return of Jesus Christ, and tremble before the prospect of the judgment of the whole earth, the examination of the works of believers and the exclusion of the ungodly from the presence of the Lord.

God is our saviour and redeemer

We believe that God made humans in his image, male and female, as the crown of creation, in order that we might live in fellowship with him. But mankind rebelled against God and fell into sin. Estranged from God yet responsible to him, sinners are subject to divine wrath, inwardly depraved, and incapable of saving themselves.

But we rejoice in God who is rich in mercy and quickened us together with Christ even though we were dead in sins. Jesus Christ is the unique and only mediator between God and mankind. There is no other name under heaven that can save us. By his life he has called us to submit to the rule of God, and by his death revealed God's love, atoned for our sins, and defeated the evil powers, thus reconciling us to God.

Having redeemed us from sin, he rose again bodily from the grave, victor over sin and death, and has ascended into heaven where he now intercedes at God's right hand for all his people and rules there as Lord of all. He has also poured out the Spirit who quickens sinners to new life in Christ, by convicting us of our sins, and leading us to repentance and faith. By the Spirit we have come to trust in the divine mercy by which we have been completely forgiven and justified freely by his grace through the merit of the cross, and have received the free gift of eternal life. In union with Christ we have been adopted into the family of God and delight to call him our father. Led by the Spirit, we are seeking to grow in the knowledge of God and in scriptural holiness, resolved to follow Christ and bear his cross in such a way that others may see our good works and glorify God in heaven.

God is calling a new community

We delight in the redeemed existence we experience as individuals and in the fellowship of the church because of God's abundant grace. By His Word and Spirit God has called us sinners out of the world into the fellowship of Christ's body which is richly endowed with spiritual gifts. We believe that the church is meant to be one, holy, universal and apostolic and we long for the day when the church drawn from every tribe and nation will be perfected and gathered before God's throne.

We believe that the church on earth is called by God to offer him acceptable worship and to serve him by the preaching of the gospel and making disciples of all nations. The flock of God is to be tended by the ministry of the Word, by means of the ordinances, the Lord's Supper and believer's baptism, and with loving pastoral care. In addition to the proclamation of the gospel, we are commanded to relieve human distress and misery, and strive for a greater measure of justice in the world.

We believe in the priesthood of all believers, in that each Christian is spiritually gifted to minister within the body of Christ and in the world. We recognize gifts of leadership and administration which are given to nurture and direct the life of the body.

We value Christian liberty, the freedom to search out the meaning of Scripture for oneself and follow the dictates of one's conscience in the fellowship of the church, and liberty for the church in the state, that the powers of this age not gain control or in any way determine our Christian obedience.

* * *

In addition to confessing our faith, I believe that we ought to defend it as well. Throughout history Christians have attended not only to the explication of the truth but to its defense also. We ought always to be ready, as Peter says, to give a reason for the hope that is in us (1 Peter 3:15). Luke wrote his two-volume work so that Theophilus might have certain knowledge about the Christian faith, and Jesus presented himself to the disciples in an unmistakable way as the risen One (Luke 1:4 Acts 1:3). We must keep in mind that one of the reasons people have rejected the biblical faith in our times is intellectual. They thought that the many objections to Christianity articulated in this century could not be answered, and therefore required a major revision of the Christian faith. If they were wrong to think so, then it is our responsibility to explain why. How is it that we evangelicals can continue to hold to the old verities in the modern age in the face of so much critical thinking? We are told not only to be teachers of sound doctrine, but also those able to refute error

(Titus 1:9). We must stop running from the modern critique of Christianity, and give more attention to the task of defending the faith. It is not only because we want to save Christianity from secular modernity. No, much more is at stake. We want to save godless people from the destruction inherent in secular modernity, both in this life and in the life to come. To do that it will be necessary, not only to witness to the gospel in the power of the Spirit, but also to think through what we are preaching and ground it in solid apologetical arguments.[19]

One of the great tragedies in Canadian church history is the fact that the centres of theological education have not been leaders in either the explication or the defense of the gospel. Our seminaries have not been places where the truth of the Bible is clearly and boldly taught, and where its historical and intellectual basis has been forthrightly defended. If anything they have been schools where faith and vision have been lost, creating a hurdle to overcome in pursuance of God's call into ministry. It is deeply tragic that the impulses of renewal seldom find support behind ivy-covered walls, and have to make their way among the people often against the pressures of academy and bureaucracy.

Of the three keys I am outlining in this book, this matter of bearing witness to the truth of the Bible is the most basic and the most difficult. It is the most basic because it underlies what to expect in the realm of spirituality and what to attempt in the area of discipleship. It is difficult because there is so much opposition to biblical faithfulness today. The relativism of our culture considers it strange and objectionable for Christians to claim a message of absolute validity. Biblical criticism operates upon the assumption that the teachings of the Bible are historically conditioned and not trans-culturally authoritative. Demythologizing takes it for granted that one can no longer believe what the New Testament says. How much easier it is to speak of spirituality and discipleship. You can always find an interest in religious feelings and social action among those who want no part of an everlasting gospel. Contempt often awaits those who say we ought to guard the gospel from false teachers. The darkest words of opprobrium are reserved for representatives of a 'historical orthodoxy', as it is called. But we must take a stand precisely here. There is a faith once delivered which is everywhere under attack even in the churches. Let us be like Timothy, touched by the Spirit, and committed to guarding the message God had given him.

A real danger today is that evangelicals may become victims of their own success. The more effective we are in communicating the everlasting gospel and the more numerous we become in the church and in society, the greater will be the pressure for us to conform to the world and accommodate our convictions to the humanistic and relativistic culture around us. We will be tempted to be jellyfish washing in and out with the tide and waves, rather than movers and shakers in our culture. We will put more value upon being accepted and respected than upon taking costly stands for God's truth. We might tend to imitate Timothy's natural timidity rather than his spiritual power in God. To be forewarned is to be forearmed.

Questions for Discussion

1. What evidence have you picked up in regard to the great defection in modern theology?
2. What is your reaction when you hear church leaders teaching contrary to the Bible?
3. What can ordinary Christians do to bring about a reformation in the churches?

For Further Reading

Donald G. Bloesch, *Essentials of Evangelical Theology* in two volumes (San Francisco: Harper & Row, 1978, 1979).

Millard J. Erickson, *Christian Theology* Vol. 1 and 2 (Grand Rapids: Baker Book House, 1983). One additional volume will appear soon.

Gabriel Fackre, *The Christ Story, A Narrative Interpretation of Basic Christian Doctrine* (Grand Rapids: Eerdmans, 1978).

J. Gresham Machen, *Christianity and Liberalism* (Grand Rapids: Eerdmans, 1923 reprint).

Thomas C. Oden, *Agenda for Theology, Recovering Christian Roots* (San Francisco: Harper & Row, 1979).

Francis A. Schaeffer, *The Great Evangelical Disaster* (Westchester: Crossway Books, 1984).

2

THE SECOND KEY:

"Walking in the Spirit"

Having begun with the key of theological identity, let us proceed to a discussion of our spiritual vitality. It is true that we have a message to preach and the duty to guard it. But unless we have appropriated it personally and can proclaim it in a demonstration of the power of the Spirit, what good is it? Dead orthodoxy is not a great deal better than heretical liberalism. Jesus told the disciples to wait in Jerusalem until they were endued with power from on high (Luke 24:49). He promised that they would receive power from God the Spirit to be Christ's witnesses to the ends of the earth (Acts 1:8).

Overcoming Dead Orthodoxy

It is not enough to believe in the whole counsel of God, if we do not experience the reality of the gospel ourselves. Mere orthodoxy cannot raise dead bones to life. Only God's breath can do that (Ezekiel 37:1-14). We have to taste the goodness of the Lord as well as declare it as a fact. God's love must be poured out into our hearts before we can credibly speak of it with our lips. After writing a marvelous doctrinal passage, the apostle turns to prayer and asks that God would help the people understand and appropriate it for themselves personally (Eph 1:15-23). In another place Paul writes: "For our gospel came to you not only in word, but also in power and in the Holy Spirit and with full conviction" (1 Thess 1:5). To be faithful to this gospel requires more than assenting intellectually to the truth — it involves also an abiding in Christ and being anointed by the Spirit of God.[1]

In my own denomination we have problems with religious liberalism in a few congregations, but a far larger problem with dead traditionalism. There are many churches where people would assent to the proper doctrine, but show no signs of spiritual life and vitality. Indeed they resist revival when it shows the slightest possibility of occurring. A revival in Wales in the last century is fine, but just begin to express need for revival now and then start to move towards it! They do not want to be part of anything which will require the placing of their lives on the altar of sacrifice or expressing their love of the Lord in unhindered ways. In short, many nominal Christians in our traditional churches today want no part of the religion of the New Testament. What kind of fidelity to the Bible is that?

Liberal churches have a problem with spiritual vitality too, but I am chiefly addressing the problem of lethargy in conservative, evangelical congregations. The reason for this is simple. If a liberal congregation wishes to know the power of the Spirit, they will need to return to the New Testament gospel of which this reality is a part. They will have to reconsider their attitude to the supernatural power of God and to the redemptive gospel of Christ. They will have some travelling to do before they can consistently face up to this New Testament doctrine. They will have to stop reducing the reality of the Spirit to the merely humanistic forces of love and relationship, and prepare themselves for an experience which will shake the foundations of their theology.[2] But those in the conservative evangelical tradition who believe the gospel intellectually are closer to the kingdom. All they have to do is to be more consistent in believing the full dimensions of the gospel they profess. They have to stop grieving and quenching the Spirit they profess to believe in. (By these remarks I am not suggesting it will be easy even for them, only that it is within their theological reach.)

It is an opportune time for us to speak of this matter. On the one hand, people are becoming more aware of the fact that New Testament religion was profoundly experiential and not just a doctrinal affair. The power of the Spirit is a hallmark of messianic faith. Had not the prophets said long ago that when the Messiah came the Spirit would be poured out? "It shall come to pass afterward, that I will pour out my Spirit on all flesh ... in those days I will pour out my Spirit." (Joel 2:28, 29) Well this is precisely what St Luke calls to our attention in his gospel by placing such emphasis upon the return of the Spirit in the birth narratives and in Acts by the prominence given to the Day of Pentecost and Peter's sermon identifying the coming of the Spirit as a fulfilment of prophecy. The power had descended, and believers were being filled with the Holy Spirit. Young and old alike were able to prophesy and praise the Lord for his mighty works (Acts 2:13, 17). One unbeliever coming into contact with a Spirit-filled congregation fell on his face and declared: "God is really among you!" (1 Cor 14:25). A good deal of the success in evangelism in the early church can be attributed to this attractive, powerful spiritual reality.

Paul too agrees with this emphasis. God's love has been poured out into our hearts (Rom 5:5). The Spirit bears witness in our spirits, and leads us to cry out "Abba! Father!" (Rom 8:16). Being filled with the Spirit makes one want to sing out in the praises of God in all kinds of ways (Eph 5:18-19). In the New Testament we are looking at high voltage Christianity, not the sad, lifeless sort of religion we are used to seeing.[3]

On the other hand, there is more of this vital religion today than there ever has been since the first century. In the twentieth century we have seen fresh impulses of the Spirit blow through the churches in what appears to be a resurgence of the primordial power of Pentecost. After the New Testament age almost everyone acknowledges a spiritual decline. Power and vitality diminish, and gifts become locked up in the clerical system. Of course the Spirit is recognized in an orthodox way, but his ministries spoken of in the New Testament are played down. The church no longer lived in the full dimension of his presence and power, his spontaneity and freedom.

The Reformation did not really confront his problem or correct it radically. Luther and Calvin concentrated upon the work of the Spirit bringing people to Christ, and did not pay enough attention to Life in the Spirit. They did not seem to grasp the dimension of the Spirit's activity which leads people to praise the Lord and spread the gospel. Nor did they do much to liberate the gifts of the Spirit distributed among all believers, but continued the clerical system. They put such a premium upon church order that they stifled any free expression of the spiritual gifts, as their successors continue to do today. They even echoed Augustine's error which claimed that God withdrew certain of the gifts with the passing of the apostles which to this writer lacks any scriptural basis and really constitutes a rationalization of a spiritual problem.

To be fair to the Reformers one should add that in their emphasis on the saving work of the Spirit they were responding to the great need of their day to clarify the gracious nature of salvation. Moreover they faced the excesses of some of the spiritualist and anabaptist groups who promoted some very questionable doctrine and practice all in the name of the Spirit. So we must not blame the Reformers too much, or be too critical of their great achievements. At the same time they do not have a lot to teach us about the renewal we now badly need.

Although there were certainly movements of the Spirit in German pietism and English methodism, it was not really until the twentieth century that we see a real breakthrough in the area of the Spirit. It began, of course, with the early Pentecostals, and then spread across practically all the denominations. The new emphasis fell where Luke had placed it on the supernatural empowering of the Spirit for living the Christian life. At first there was strong opposition to it, but as the years went by the movement grew and began to affect other groups. Then in mid-century a new manifestation of Pentecost took place in the traditional denominations, even in the most traditional of all, the Catholic church, resulting today in the most vigorous forms of ministry and piety which have become a dominant reality in the modern church. Even though some of this charismatic movement is surely spurious and affected, much of it is not, and must be considered by a fair-minded Christian as a rejuvenation of the pentecostal reality.

I do not think that Rodman Williams exaggerates when he speaks of a 'new era' in church history. An extraordinary spiritual renewal is occurring across Christendom, especially in the third world. We are seeing a release of spiritual dynamism which knows no denominational limits. People are being caught up in a modern expression of Pentecost which promises to revive the entire church, and may even lead to a fulfilment of our mission to the world. For this we hope and pray.[4]

So it is a good time to take a look at what God has for us in the realm of the Spirit.

Joyful zeal in serving the Lord

There are many images of the church in the New Testament. It is called the body of Christ, the people of God, the bride of Christ, and so on. These images tell us what God meant the church to be and become. One major image of the church which concerns us here is that of the *temple of the Lord.* Of the church Paul says, "the whole structure is joined together and grows into a holy temple in the Lord, in whom you are also built into it for a dwelling place of God in the Spirit" (Eph 2:21-22). In the same vein Peter says that we are stones built into 'a spiritual house' to be a holy priesthood and to offer up appropriate sacrifices to God through Jesus Christ (1 Peter 2:4-5). In other words, the church is the place where God is present in power and reality and wanting to be greeted with joyful praise and thanksgiving. How easily we forget what 'serving the Lord' used to mean. Not just performing duties on behalf of God, but actually ministering to God himself! When we praise and adore our wonderful God, we minister to him and gladden his heart. God is glorified when his people minister to him with the adoration which springs from a spiritually renewed heart. As Isaiah said, "This people have I formed for myself — they shall show forth my praise" (43:7). God wants us to love him for himself and not just for the gifts he has given to us. We should not even try to minister for the Lord in the church and in the world until we have been ministering to the Lord as priests in his holy temple.

Wasn't this the obvious secret of the early church? She delighted in the presence of God, and out of that exuberant fulness the power flowed. Out of the rich experience of the presence of God the people overflowed in praise, in mission, and in service of every kind. The 'body' of Christ in those days was healthy in all its vital signs. The life of God surged through the arteries, and gave life to all the members. The believers expected God to act, and he did. They praised God with joy and radiant faces. The love for God and neighbour poured forth. There was power in their witness and authority in spiritual things. The gospel was not dead doctrine to them, but experientially alive and vital orthodoxy. And the church was zealous for the good works God planned for her to be doing. Out of that inward life, born of the Spirit, all these good fruits grew and flourished, as they will also today if we behave like God's temple and Spirit-filled people.

By way of caution let me add two points. First, such an experience of revival will not lift us up above the experience of cross-bearing and pain altogether. There are some who give the impression that being filled with the Spirit means painless and prosperous Christianity. It is not so. As Paul says, "We who have the firstfruits of the Spirit groan inwardly as we wait for adoption as sons, the redemption of our bodies" (Rom 8:23). The Spirit will enable us to face fiery trials, but he will not always shield us from them. Second, we must be aware that when revival happens, the Enemy creates counterfeit forms of it. The flesh finds all sorts of new ways to express itself, in forms of pride and rivalry and separatism. Revival is not a panacea for the problems of the church. It may well have greater problems under revival than it had before! Nevertheless, the church must seek to be alive unto God whatever the cost. It ought to long that God would do in our day the things he used to do.

As we have noted, however, the church has not been too eager for revival to come. Early in Christian history church leaders got nervous about permitting freedom in the Spirit for fear of false prophecy and uncontrolled enthusiasm. So they clamped down upon Christian freedom and placed it firmly beneath a strong hierarchical order. They deliberately chose form over freedom, order over spontaneity. They did not welcome the Spirit moving in their midst in ways not anticipated by their blueprints. They opted for a largely Spirit-less church, a church whose corporate life would resemble a funeral parlour rather than a temple of praise. And, by the working of the law of logical consequences, they got what they asked for. They produced Christians who are shy about God, who have trouble talking excitedly about God to non-Christians or even fellow-Christians. Not very much is happening in their lives, and if they are forced to give a testimony they have to reach back a couple of decades to come up with something to share. They have the form of godliness but not the power. They would be shocked if somebody jumped up in the church service to share what God is doing and saying, or just to praise God's name. People seem to be in church to hear a formal lecture, and not to celebrate God. Joyful celebration is about the last thing they would feel comfortable doing. How odd it is that a Baptist tradition like mine is actually more at home in the Catholic liturgical stream where everything is written down and predictable and feel very ill at ease when someone suggests that we should actually practice the priesthood of all believers! Of course we would say that the church is a temple of the Spirit of God, but don't let the service go more than an hour and don't allow anything to happen that is unplanned. For all our formal claims, most of our Protestant churches are as unlike the New Testament pattern as most Catholic churches are.

No wonder little is happening. The saints are circulating among the churches, but how many people are really being converted from unbelief in Canada? Very few in the average congregation. Why is that? There cannot be effective evangelism where the Spirit is quenched. Why? Because the most important factor in reaching people for Christ is the quality of our corporate life in him. We cannot share the life if we do not have it. People will not be attracted to God if his people are not joyful in his presence. Effective evangelism is an expression of renewal. When the church is caught up in the praise and love of God, outsiders start to ask what is going on. Preaching then comes as an answer to the question raised by the joyful praise of the people. Faith is more caught than taught, and is a contagion picked up from those who delight in their Saviour. True evangelism is relatively simple. It comes from the overflow of the life of God in his people. If there is not obvious life among us, there will be no believers who will want to share and no unbelievers who will care to listen.[5]

Plainly we need a revival to come sweeping over our congregations. It is not enough to love God by an act of the will when we can love him with our whole heart. It is good to *believe* that God is with us, but even better to *know* that he is with us. Sharing our faith is a duty given to us by Christ, but how much better when it arises out of the Spirit of God in the churches so that we will be freed up to worship and magnify him.[6]

How can we have such a revival? Of course we cannot create it for ourselves at will. It will take a miracle of God. Nevertheless, God's Word tells us what God loves and has promised to bless. We know what he honours and does not honour. Thus there are actions we can take to prepare for his visitation. *First*, we must really desire revival. We must ask God to give it to us. "You have not because you ask not" (James 4:2). We must be serious with God about it, and implore him in prayer to bless his people. *Second*, there must be heartfelt repentance. God does not hear our prayers if our iniquities have made a separation between us (Isaiah 59:1-2). He will not answer us if we provoke him to his face. A holy God cannot bless a wicked people. Therefore, we must face up to the ways in which we have allowed ourselves to be squeezed into the world's mould and lived according to the flesh rather than the Spirit. We have to face up to the reasons we are in the condition we are in, and bring forth works worthy of repentance. God says through Malachi that if the people attend to their duties to God he will open the windows of heaven and pour out an overflowing blessing (Malachi 3:10). *Third*, we must stop neglecting and possibly quenching the Spirit of God and allow him to have his freedom among us. There must be a yieldedness to God's breath blowing where it wills. The Spirit is not just a doctrine, he is a person who can be experienced as leading, teaching, and empowering us. We have to ask him to fill us, and to work in our midst in new ways.

One thing in particular we must look at is our traditional order of service. It just will not do to plan them down to the last detail and then expect the Spirit to have any freedom. We will be prevented from experiencing the fulness of the Spirit if we continue to depend upon a one-man ministry and a rigid pattern of worship. We have to become more flexible so that the Spirit will have some room to move. What if God wants to change the flow of the service and to speak through some lowly saint — when will this be possible? What if there is a person who desperately needs prayer but there is no natural way to do that because of our tight agenda? What if God wants to indicate a new course of action while the people are ministering to him — how is this to happen? The world missionary movement began in a service where in the midst of the praise and preaching the word came to set apart Barnabas and Saul for God's work (Acts 13:2). Is it not a sobering thought that this could not have happened in ninety percent of our churches today? Let us set our traditions beneath the Word of God and surrender them to the Spirit of God, and let Jesus be Lord in our midst.

Renewal in the Gifts of the Spirit

As the body of Christ, the church is also equipped with a wonderful range of spiritual gifts. In each person, we are told, the Spirit manifests himself in unique ways (1 Cor 12:7). These gifts are given to build up the church and to enable it to minister to the world. The church is not meant to be determined by a clerical structure but by a gift structure. Every believer, a priest of God, and gifted to serve God. There is a wonderful diversity of these gifts — some of them are spectacular, while others are ordinary and everyday phenomena. And every believer receives God's gift or gifts, and not only a special group or class. We could say, indeed we must say, that the church is a charismatic community which is meant to function in the gifts of God's Spirit. Each person is called by God to exercise a particular ministry in the congregation. The church is an egalitarian community, each person is gifted by God.

One obvious implication of this is that we must be done with clericalism. God does not want the church to be dominated by the ego and gifts of one person. He wants the whole body involved in ministry which means each believer is expected to exercise his/her gift. Does this mean we will not need ministers any more? Not at all. On the contrary, they will be needed more than ever. They will be busy nurturing and enabling people in their gifts and ministries, and exercising oversight upon a liberated congregational life. Such oversight will certainly be more demanding not less than before.

Earlier I referred to a decline in spiritual vitality when the clamps were placed upon the freedom of the Spirit to work in the churches. One of the effects of this action was to close the minds and hearts of believers to the full range of spiritual gifts available according to the New Testament. People began to have limited expectations as to the possibilities in this area, and as a result manifestations of the Spirit began to decline. This led to a general impoverishment in the worship of the church and the spiritual lives of its members.

This is very obvious today. Large numbers of Christians are simply not open to certain gifts of the Spirit. They are suspicious and afraid of them. If they encounter tongues, they suspect false tongues. If they hear a prophecy, they worry about false prophecy. If they encounter prayer for the sick, they mumble about miracle-mongering. To put it in a word, we are *un*believing when it comes to this aspect of New Testament teaching. Let us say that there is a range of gifts in the New Testament from A to Z. Well, we seem to be open to gifts A to P but not gifts R to Z. Whereas the early church was open to the full range of gifts, we are not. We place a limit on what God can give us. We do not take seriously the possibility that God may want to give us gifts belonging to the forbidden group of our tradition. And since God usually takes us where we are, he deals with us according to our limited faith, and does not waste the gifts on us.

This is a tragic situation, all the more because it is not recognized as such. Without any good reason except fear, we are putting a limit on what God can do among us. We accept the gift of teaching, and refuse the gift of prophecy. We accept the gift of preaching and refuse the gifts of prayer-language. We accept the gifts of mercy and refuse to ask for miracles. We study books and ignore dreams and visions. Instead of repenting for the ways in which we have grieved the Spirit with a high hand, we go on explaining why we do with specious arguments.

Yes, Paul says that prophecy and tongues will cease, but not until the coming of the Lord when they will not be needed. Until that time they are needed and serve the community on its pilgrimage here below (1 Cor 13:8-13). Far from proving a cessation of certain gifts, what Paul says underlines the crucial importance of all the gifts God in his sovereignty is pleased to give us. Imagine what it would be like if a church refused the gift of teaching. They would probably get into all kinds of erroneous doctrine and strange ideas, lacking the control which sound teaching provides. But what about the churches which refuse the gift of prophecy? Are they not lacking in something too? Are they not forfeiting the privilege of hearing those fresh promptings of the Spirit who wants to get through to them? who wants to speak to them through prophets who are in intimate contact with him? The church in which teaching is missing will be a chaotic place, but a church where prophecy is missing will be a place where the Spirit is quenched. "Do not quench the Spirit, do not despise prophesying, but test everything" (1 Thess 5:19-20). What we have done in order to prevent the unpredictable from happening is to allow the church to fall into the pattern of a pastor-dominated hierarchical congregation in which the leading of the Spirit is suppressed.[7]

I suspect that the greatest hindrance to renewal in this area is our fear of the unknown. We worry about what other people will think of us. We worry about what God might do if we were radically open to him. We want to have things under control and hence we worry about situations in which the agenda is left open for the Spirit to lead and move. If fear is our problem, we had better deal with it directly. If the Holy Spirit is in, blueprints are out. If we want him to lead us, we must stop giving all the directions to ourselves. There has to be a letting go. There has to be openness and expectancy in the presence of the Spirit who is free to act when and where he wills.

Just to get a feeling for what is missing in the church today in the area of gifts, let us run through one of Paul's lists where most of them are mentioned:

1 Corinthians 12:8-10

i "the utterance of wisdom" Paul makes reference here to the wisdom from on high which God sometimes gives to us when we ask for it (James 1:5). Exemplified in the book of Proverbs, this would be an insight into the best course of action to take in some challenge facing the church family, whether it be a matter of ethical, doctrinal, or ordinary leading.

ii "the utterance of knowledge" The focus of this gift is likely to be insight into the meaning of salvation and the Word of God. The Spirit who searches the depths of God is willing to share insight with us on how to move in interpretation and application. The gift is often seen in great teachers of the faith who possess remarkable insight into God's intention lying behind a given text or passage.

iii "faith" Paul is not thinking here of saving faith which all Christians exercise, but of mountain-removing faith (1 Cor 13:2). It is the kind of extraordinary confidence in God which enables an Elijah to take on all the prophets of Baal single-handed. This surge of confidence in God appears in the next two gifts as well.

iv "gifts of healings" In healing a confidence is experienced which enables one to pray for healing and then see it happen. As James says, "the prayer of faith shall heal the sick" (James 5:16). In such an event the powers of death are temporarily rolled back and the resurrection power of Jesus is seen. Complete healing is only ours at the resurrection of the body, but in the meantime special healings can occur according to the sovereign will of God.

v "the working of miracles" This gift is the confidence to ask for the intervention of God in miraculous ways outside of healing. The apostles asked for it when they prayed that God would prevent their enemies from harming them when it was well within their power to do so (Acts 4:29). Of course we are not in a position to demand a miracle and cannot dictate to God what he must do. But we can look to him for acts of deliverance and blessing when these are necessary and can hope that he will do it.

vi "prophecy" The gift of prophecy is not the same as the gift of teaching. Both build up the church, but in different ways. In prophecy an insight is articulated which was not prepared for by study or effort. At Antioch it was undoubtedly a prophecy which alerted the people to God's will in regard to Barnabas and Saul becoming the first missionaries. Prophecy opens the church up to a teaching ministry of the Spirit which complements but does not supplant the regular planned and prepared teaching office. Its hallmark is the immediacy with which the message comes under the prompting of the Spirit.

vii "The ability to distinguish between spirits" This gift can be paired with prophecy. Indeed it is used in discerning whether a prophecy is genuine or not. It enables people to weigh what the prophet says and determine whether God gave the word in question (1 Cor 14:29). It parallels somewhat the relation of interpretation to the gift of tongues. I see it operating in the apostle Paul when he perceived that Elymas the magician was doing Satan's work (Acts 13:8-9), and also when Paul could see the spirit of faith in the cripple at Lystra and therefore told him to stand on his feet. It wasn't so much that Paul healed the lame man, as that Paul discerned that the man possessed faith that he could be healed (Acts 14:9). Its importance for theology is very plain from what John says: "Beloved, do not believe every spirit, but test the spirits to see whether they are of God, for many false prophets have gone out into the world" (1 John 4:1). In modern theology, as we have noticed in chapter one, the gift of discerning spirits, including the lies of the Devil, is absolutely indispensable.

viii "various kinds of tongues" It is quite clear from 1 Cor 14 that the gift of tongues is the gift of a prayer-language. Paul calls it praying in the Spirit, and differentiates it from praying with the mind in the normal way (14:14-16). In tongues one can communicate with God in an effective way, particularly concerning matters whether of praise or intercession which are hard to put into speech. In this kind of prayer the believer is able to transcend the normal limits of speech-determined prayer and soar in the heavenlies.

ix "the interpretation of tongues" This gift is obviously a complement to the gift of tongues and makes it available to the larger group. Tongues cannot edify the church unless and until they are interpreted. "Therefore, he who speaks in a tongue should pray for the power to interpret" (1 Cor 14:13). Ordinarily this is done by someone else, and amounts to a sense of what is being prayed in the tongue. It is less a translation of it, in my opinion, and more of a feeling of its impulse and direction.

By reviewing such a list, we can understand the problem better, namely that the average Christian today is not fully aware of these gifts and not skilled in operating within this context: What can be done about this?

First, we must rid ourselves of a false fear of God and what he may want to give us. We have to trust the One who gives liberally and does not demand too much from his servants. Second, we must see that God's people are properly informed and instructed in the gift possibilities which belong to them as the body of Christ. They need to be taught in the Scriptures, exposed to gifts operating in other assemblies, and encouraged to experiment with gifts the Lord may be giving them. Third, there has to be wise pastoral oversight. Coping with a charismatic renewal at Corinth, Paul had to give the believers there a good deal of advice on how to handle the situation. He told them that uninterpreted tongues would not help the congregation. But then he added that they should not forbid speaking in tongues in proper ways. Paul encouraged them to prophesy, but had to say that people should only do so one at a time and then under the scrutiny of the others in the church. In particular Paul insisted that unless gifts mediate love to others, they were worse than useless. And he stressed that no one gift put anyone in a superior position to others (1 Cor 12-14).

The point is that pastoral problems always arise where the gifts of the Spirit are freely exercised. Let me refer to some of the abuses we are familiar with today. Some claim that unless you speak in tongues you have not received the fulness of the Spirit of which tongues is the normative sign. The same people often hold that healing is always the will of God, and that if a person is not healed there must be something wrong with him/her. Frequently one meets with a kind of charismania which puts enormous emphasis on the extraordinary gifts and miraculous occurrences as if the everyday working of God were somehow inferior to that. Now these sort of erroneous opinions are the result of poor teaching from the New Testament and are propagated by sect-like agencies in books, magazines, tapes, and TV. And they can cause harm in individuals who believe them and split whole congregations. It is the Enemy sowing tares among the wheat and we must not let him get away with it. Satan is always eager to discredit true revival by spreading false revival in the midst of it. What a tragedy it would be if in seeking to stamp out the false fire we quenched the Spirit of God as well. Let us at all costs avoid a polarization between those who want no renewal of any kind and those who want revival with excess and aberration. Surely we all want what God has for us as indicated in his Word because we need it for the work of the ministry we have been given.

Be filled with the Holy Spirit!

Let us now discuss how individuals can be renewed in the Spirit. At the outset let us remember that the Spirit in the New Testament was an experience not a doctrine. He was known in the pouring out of God's love into people's hearts. You experienced him in the impulse you felt to cry 'Abba! Father!' You felt his power when you shared the gospel with anointing and unction. You saw him doing miracles among the congregation (Gal 3:5). New Testament Christianity was experientially rich. The reality of God flooded the lives of believers.

The problem is that this is not always true today. Large numbers of Christians have not experienced the truth at this point and cannot identify with the pentecostal experience of the New Testament. Of course we know that the Spirit indwells all those who confess that Jesus Christ is Lord (1 Cor 12:3). So these Christians do not lack the potential for experiencing God in the normative scriptural way. But they do lack an actual sense of the presence and grace of God, and a strong faith in what God is able to do. In part, it is not their fault. What can one expect if 'lay-people' have been conditioned to sit still and listen and never enter energetically into the blessings God has for them? They resemble the disciples whom Jesus told to wait in Jerusalem until the power comes from on high (Luke 24:49). Even though they are by status living after Pentecost, they are not living after it in fact. They are not tasting the goodness of the Lord.

This fact is particularly tragic because we desperately need Christians to be empowered by the Spirit if we are ever going to get the job done God has given us. Unbelievers will not be saved and North America will not be shaken by the law of God unless we are alive in the Spirit and committed without reservation. The church needs Christians who have been touched by God, those for whom prayer is not a tedious formality but a way of life. We need believers for whom God is real, and God's Word precious, people who love one another and want to serve the Lord, whose hearts are aflame with vision and zeal.

But the truly wonderful thing to report about twentieth-century Christianity is that more people than ever before are testifying to a fresh touch of God on their lives. Everywhere you turn you encounter a story of how someone entered into a fuller dimension of the Spirit which proved to be life-transforming for him. Not conversion as such, but a new way of God's working in the individual.

It happened to me in 1967 in New Orleans. I was a young theologian, heavily into intellectual reflection as I am now, but feeling a lack of reality and power which comes from an unbalanced life. Although Paul plainly says we should use both mind and spirit, theologians generally exercise only the mind. One day Dorothy and I were invited to a home prayer fellowship meeting at 9 o'clock in the evening after church. We went along and found a group of about a dozen people chatting over coffee. As the meeting began, it was obvious that God was very real and much loved by these people. Each of them would refer to things God had done for them that week, and express their hope for answers to prayer in the coming few days. These people were alive unto God, as Paul says. When we got down to praying for one another and for specific items of need, the time flew by. People were eager to pray and expressed great joy and faith in the presence of the Lord. I was touched by God that night. I glimpsed the dimension of the Spirit which the New Testament describes but is so often absent in churches today. The Bible came alive to me in this and in other respects. Being a Christian became an exciting adventure instead of a drag. I was filled with the Spirit.

Michael Cassidy, the founder of African Enterprise, had the mountain-top experience in 1977. An active evangelical leader, Cassidy was familiar with the New Testament and the doctrine of the Spirit. He knew all the reasons why the Pentecostals were wrong, and felt he had the issue settled in his mind. But he knew there was something missing. The breakthrough occurred when he attended some meetings in Johannesburg. The people were alive with praise and rejoicing. God's presence was unmistakable and Michael knew it was the time to surrender to him. Back in his room that night the spirit of praise began to rise in his soul. Hour after hour he uttered the praises of God in unrestrained doxology and song. The Spirit bubbled up from deep within him. All through the night he went on praising the Lord, and when the new day broke it was luminous with God's light and love. God had brought Michael Cassidy into his presence and touched his life in an unmistakable way.[8]

Scripture scholar George T. Montague likens it to riding the wind. He had been raised in a traditional Christian home and gone on to study theology. He knew the theory very well and was vaguely aware of needing to experience God more fully. He went to a prayer meeting where God was present to check it out, and there was released within him a stream of life which had been held back for years. He stopped trying to prevent it from flowing and what happened was a welling up of the Spirit of God from within. "I began to feel, for the first time in my life, like the buzzards I had as a child watched gliding in the sky for hours without flapping their wings — they let the wind carry them."[9]

It is an exciting time to be a Christian. Something is taking place in every corner of the church to renew the body of Christ. We are seeing a revival happening through the power of the Holy Spirit. God may have seemed absent before, but now he is a compelling presence. In many churches there is a new mood of praise and thanksgiving to God. People are feeling the peace and joy of the Lord in new ways. The old denominational divisions are beginning to break down under the power of the ecumenical Spirit of God who works in all Christian believers. The Bible has become a new book, and things are starting to happen in people's lives. Healing, prophecy, and tongues are beginning to operate again, and there is a mood of openness and expectancy in the air. We believe the same gospel truths as we did before, but now the truths are becoming operational. They are starting to mean more than they did before experientially. We are all the children of God, but now we are feeling the freedom in our sonship. The gospel is both true and real — we have been touched by the presence of God!

What shall we call what has been happening to these people? In a sense it doesn't matter very much. Some are comfortable calling it a baptism in the Spirit because it is an empowering immersion in the Spirit like that which Luke spoke about. On the day of Pentecost Jesus baptized the church with the Spirit and gave them power to be his witnesses (Acts 1:5, 8 2:1-4). But others point out that there are problems with this nomenclature. Baptism into Christ by the Spirit is something which happens when we accept the Lord and not something that happens much later (Acts 2:38 10:45). What we are describing is obviously not conversion but an enrichment in Christian experience. To call it a baptism would be to suggest that people did not even have the Spirit before this experience.

On the other hand, there are those who insist that what they have experienced is what Luke describes as a baptism in power so it must be all right to call it that. Why be so uptight about what we call it when the real issue is the experience itself? What good is it to claim a baptism in the Spirit, meaning conversion, if the experiential reality is not there? Let us not fight about a name when what we need is an awakening to new life and effectiveness.

My own preference is to speak of the infilling of the Spirit, and to see it as a realization of what is already ours potentially in Christ. This fits both the exegetical requirements of the New Testament and the reality of modern experience of the Spirit. Conversion is indeed a baptism in the Spirit, but after that it may be necessary to experience the fulness of what that blessing promises. God does not limit himself to our tidy doctrinal schemes. He wants to fill people with his love and power whatever language we use. We must not try to put him into a straightjacket. The Spirit blows where it will. He does not read our rubrics and will not be bound to our agendas. He wants to set us free. Arguing over nomenclature can be no more than a tactic of avoiding an encounter with him.

The question you must ask yourself is this: am I alive unto God? have I experienced the fruit of my conversion? do I have an anointing from God? do I really love the Lord and his Word? If you are unsure, then stop arguing over terms and start yielding your life to God so that he may fill you with his Spirit.[10]

We have an energy crisis in the churches of North America. There is a low level of spiritual power evident in the lives of so many Christians. We need a fresh impulse of power for ministry and the life of faith. There are too many dead preachers giving dead sermons to dead congregations. We need the Spirit of God to come sweeping over this valley of dead bones.

But what can I do personally to experience spiritual renewal in my own life? First, you have to be serious about wanting it. The risen Lord condemned the churches of Sardis and Laodicea for being dead and lukewarm in their commitment. It was their fault that they were not renewed. They had grieved the Spirit and quenched his power in different ways, and had to come to terms with that fact and repent (Rev 3:1-6, 14-22). Are you perhaps to blame for the fact that your spiritual vitality level is low? Are you serious about giving your life over to God without reservation?

Second, we know that God wants to give the Spirit to those who ask him (Luke 11:13). You will not be asking God for something he is unwilling to give. He stands at the door and knocks, wanting to come in. Do not be afraid of yielding to him. Trust him in this, and then wait for the renewal to manifest itself in you. It will not be exactly the same for every one. The rushing wind and tongues of fire have not been repeated since Pentecost to my knowledge. We cannot put the Spirit in a box. Sometimes renewal is manifest and occurs at a very definite moment. The person is overwhelmed by the presence, power, and love of God. He may speak in tongues or he may not, but the experience of peace and great joy is unmistakable. But in other cases the renewal is more hidden. It is not marked by a dramatic experience or charismatic sign and at first the person may wonder if anything happened at all. But after a few days he begins to realize that something did indeed happen to him. Light has dawned in his soul although he did not notice the sunrise at the time. The peace and joy come, not like an avalanche, but like rising waters gradually permeating his whole being. As time goes on one becomes certain that God has touched his or her life. Whether manifest or hidden, this renewal in the Spirit can have the character of a new beginning to a life more under the impulse and control of the Spirit of God. You will be able to say with the psalmist, "My cup runneth over" (Psalm 23:5).

Third, it may be useful to consult with another Christian about this matter. Recall that at Samaria the Spirit was given in connection with the laying on of hands (Acts 8:14). Now this is not a necessity — many receive the Spirit without any such action. But it is still true that the Spirit indwells his temple, the church, and wants us to be living stones in that building. Therefore, the Spirit uses people already renewed to help people who desire renewal. Ananias was sent to Paul to minister healing and the coming of the Spirit (Acts 9:17). The Spirit came upon the disciples at Ephesus after Paul laid his hands upon them (19:6). So it is quite possible that you ought to go to a person you are sure is renewed in the Spirit and ask them to pray for you to receive the Spirit in power. I did that myself, and believe God used it. Normally if you want to be filled with the Spirit, you should go to a community of Christians who are filled and ask for their help.

Now there are dangers in what we are talking about. The fallen flesh will seek to manifest itself in us whether we are spiritually alive or lukewarm. Satan will not cease to try to spoil the work of God. The detractors of renewal can always point to defects and excesses and use them to cast doubt on the renewal. For example, elitism is a common problem. People who have come into renewal can easily see themselves as a superior class within the church and look down upon other Christians as carnal. In actual fact of course renewal is not the guarantee of Christian maturity or holiness and not a reason for despising other members of Christ's body. Fanaticism can also happen. Because of the renewed sense of the Spirit's presence, people may assume that their thoughts are God's thoughts and that they are enlightened directly from on high. They can even appeal to the Spirit in an attempt to cover their own wickedness or folly. The truth can always be distorted or misused. Separatism is another problem. Those who have received the Spirit may think of themselves as superior as a group and despise the ordinary Christianity of the local church. They may reject church authority and separate to form a new sect.

Nevertheless, dangers or not, we need to experience a fuller sense of what it means to be the Spirit-filled people of God both as individuals and as congregations. I believe that God has more for us than we have been willing to receive. We have claimed to be open to the reviving work of God as this was manifested in the past. But we have tended to resist the signs of revival when they have actually occurred. We have been so alarmed by the possible abuses of the Spirit that we have become abnormally timid about his possible uses. I believe that God is calling his whole church to a fuller realization of what it means to have received the Holy Spirit. I hope that the mighty work of God now going on will impact beneficially upon all of our church traditions, and that we will set our hearts on moving in this direction and handle such problems as may arise maturely and with scriptural sense.

Of course we cannot make revival happen. God must visit and redeem his people in power. But let us not be too modest. God has told us in his Word what he loves and what he hates, what he will bless and not bless. He has told us what we ought to do. After God gave the promise to make the desolate land like the Garden of Eden, he said: "This also I will let the house of Israel ask me to do for them" (Ezek 36:37). God wants us to turn to him, to forsake our sins, and call upon his name. "If my people who are called by my name humble themselves and pray and seek my face and turn from their evil ways, then I will hear from heaven, and will forgive their sin and heal their land" (2 Chron 7:14).

There are several reasons why revival may tarry. But one of them is certainly the fear that prevents us from being radically open to the Spirit of God. God has so much more for us than we have been willing to accept; let us cast off our fears and get down to serious prayer that the holy breath of God will come sweeping over us. God wants to do miracles in our midst. He wants us to worship him with freedom, to experience the truth of the Bible in fresh ways, and to be able to share the gospel in a more effective and natural manner. The church will not come alive or become effective by human ingenuity or planning, but only by an inundation of the Spirit. Let us not settle for the low-level of spirituality and commitment which sadly are characteristic of the modern churches, but let us drop to our knees and ask God to give all he has for us. Then I believe it can come true in the spiritual realm what Isaiah said: "Once more God will send us his Spirit. The wasteland will become fertile, and the fields will produce rich crops" (32:15).

In closing, let me give you a word of prophecy: "My people, says the Lord, incline unto me. Be not afraid but trust in me. I want to do among you the wonderful things I used to do. Believe in me. Call on me to do it for you."

Questions for Discussion

1. Do you see evidence of spiritual renewal today?
2. What is the greatest hindrance to revival?
3. What is the outlook towards renewal in your church or denomination?

For Further Reading

Michael Green, *I Believe in the Holy Spirit* (Grand Rapids: Eerdmans, 1975)

Alisdair Heron, *The Holy Spirit, In the Bible, The History of Christian Thought, and Recent Theology* (Philadelphia: the Westminster Press, 1983)

Charles E. Hummel, *Fire in the Fireplace, Contemporary Charismatic Renewal* (Downers Grove: Inter Varsity Press, 1978)

Richard F. Lovelace, *Dynamics of Spiritual Life, An Evangelical Theology of Renewal* (Downers Grove: Inter Varsity Press, 1979)

George Mallone, *Those Controversial Gifts* (Downers Grove: Inter Varsity Press, 1983)

George T. Montague, *The Holy Spirit, Growth of a Biblical Tradition* (New York: Paulist Press, 1976)

3

THE THIRD KEY:

"Obeying the Lord"

Being faithful to God involves even more than holding fast to the message of the Bible and being open to the Spirit. There is also a lifestyle requirement. If we believe the Bible, we must obey the commandments of God. And if we have new life from the Spirit, we must also walk in the Spirit. There is no way that we can be faithful to God if we ignore God's will in the ethical realm. There is no getting around the fact that we have been called to take up Christ's cross and follow him.

The reason God gave us the gospel message and poured out his Spirit upon us was to facilitate the coming of his kingdom and the doing of his will on earth as in heaven. God wants a 'people zealous for good works' (Titus 2:14). His Word tells us what we ought to be doing, and his Spirit empowers us in doing righteousness. New life is meant to lead to a new lifestyle. "We were buried with him by baptism unto death, so that as Christ was raised from the dead by the glory of the Father, we too might walk in newness of life" (Rom 6:4).

God does not want a doctrinally impeccable church which is turned in upon itself, or a euphoric church which is preoccupied with its emotional highs. He wants people who believe his Word and are open to his Spirit in order to disciple the nations and bring God's righteousness to bear upon all of culture. Far from being a substitute for the gospel, this act of obedience in world mission and reclamation is the proper expression of the gospel. "Go therefore and make disciples of all nations."

Agenda for Biblical People

What then are the ethical imperatives of the faith? What prophetic note does the Bible sound? What issues ought we to attend to?[1]

The first and basic note is sounded in the creation narrative. God called us, male and female, to fill the earth and subdue it, and to have dominion over everything (Genesis 1:26-30). Humans were made in God's image, personal agents such as God is, in order to represent God in the visible realm and extend his rule over the creation. We are the stewards of creation, responsible to God for our stewardship. Not to try to exercise dominion is to disobey the command of God. Since the fall into sin, and the introduction of disorder into the world, the dominion mandate also involves restoration and winning back what was lost. Religion covers all our activities as we seek to manage and use what has been given to the glory of God.

In order to achieve the redemption of mankind and the reclamation of the culture, God called Abraham and his descendants to serve him. The idea was to create a new people who would be responsive to God's covenant and live in accord with God's will. Israel would be a light to the nations by virtue of the fact that it would live not in conformity with this fallen age but by the will of God. Thus God decided to form a distinctive community with its own special standards of behaviour which would incarnate God's will for humankind.

In order to spell out in detail the nature of God's will for individual and communal life a law was given through Moses. In it we find general, moral and legal principles as well as numerous specific commandments designed to direct the life of Israel. As the One who created the universe and called Israel to be his people, God was in a position to give his law to them as the foundation of wisdom. "Keep them and do them, for that will be your wisdom and your understanding in the sight of the peoples" (Deut 4:6). God gave Israel a blueprint for the execution of the dominion covenant in a fallen situation.

Jesus endorsed the law of God in the strongest possible terms, and went on to expound upon it (Matt 5:17-19). Not only God's eternal nature, but God's will for mankind was incarnate in him. Jesus preached the coming of the kingdom of God which included a vision of what life under God would be like. He invited people to participate in the new order which was dawning in him and called together a new community which would live according to the kingdom. Both by his life and in his teachings, Jesus deepened our understanding of what God in his law requires. He placed great emphasis upon responding to those in any kind of need and devoted a good deal of his attention to shaping a new kind of human being. He told us not to be slaves of possessions, not to seek vengeance, not to grasp for power, not to turn away from the poor and the afflicted.

How we ought to live continues to be a lively subject in the epistles as well. Our manner of life, Paul says, ought to be worthy of the gospel of Christ (Phil 1:27). This would involve, he goes on to say, acting in humility and love towards our brothers and sisters. All the themes of Jesus turn up again in the epistles: love of the neighbour, compassion toward the weak, the forgiveness of enemies, liberation from possessions. We are to yield our lives to God as a living sacrifice and not hold anything back. Two of the three tests of a true Christian in First John are lifestyle tests. In addition to believing the gospel of the incarnation, Christians must obey God's commandments and love one another (1 John 2:3 3:14). The gospel calls for both a belief-response and an action-response.

We live before God in the sure and certain hope of the coming of the kingdom and the victory of Christ. Our future is not blocked. There can be no question of defeat. We look forward to the day when the nations will all have been baptized and discipled, and when the laws of God will be observed everywhere. Blessings will flow from the godless to the godly and earth's cultures will be transformed. God's kingdom has already broken in, and Satan has been defeated. It is only a matter of time until the leaven shall leaven the whole lump and the knowledge of the Lord will cover the earth as the waters cover the sea. The heritage of the nations will be given to the Lord's anointed, and Christ will reign forever and ever.[2]

Being Christian in a Pagan Society

The biblical agenda can be divided into two parts: the challenge to us as individuals to live the Christian life, and the challenge to the church to reclaim the culture for God. Both of them are demanding, but the second is the most controversial and needs the most attention.

As far as individual lifestyle goes, the challenge is to act like Christians in an increasingly secularized social order. The reason for this is the same as the one which makes orthodox theology hard to affirm for some modern people. We face in secularist modernity a godless orientation to life which makes it harder than it used to be to behave in distinctively Christian ways. At one time in the West there was a Christian consensus within which it seemed plausible to act like a Christian even if you were not one. But nowadays not only can the biblical value system not be taken for granted — it is under great pressure and even attack. Christians exist in a new secular environment which demands that we assimilate or disappear. We are seeing Western culture dechristianized and the lines clearly drawn between biblical people and unbelievers.

Let me list a few of the trends in modern society which put the pressure on the Christian ethos. First, there is the breakup of natural groupings such as the family and smaller communities and their replacement by enormous pluralistic cities and purely functional relationships. With the weakening of these groupings, the normal and natural way of passing on Christian faith and values is threatened and the authority of the secular realm takes over. Second, specialization and the knowledge explosion have greatly enhanced the technical side of modern life but they have also cut into one's sense of competence of confidence in what we know. We find ourselves having to refer to expert opinion constantly to be sure of anything. In the area of religion and ethics this means depending on people who very often study the subjects from a supposedly scientific angle leaving faith out of it. Thus faith and behaviour undergo the same process of secularization as is occurring in the wider society. Secular experts become the real authority even for Christians, not scripture, tradition, or church leadership. Third, the all-pervasive media constitutes another problem for us. The media dominate our thinking and comprise the source of much of our information and therefore attitudes, yet they are controlled by secular influences for the most part. Our young people are being taught a way of life from an alien source of authority. Right in our own homes they are bombarded with secular values which far exceed the teaching input of Sunday School or family devotions if any. Fourth, statist education shapes all our children who attend public schools. No longer are children brought up by godly parents and an attentive church — they are shaped by a secular teaching staff working from a secular curriculum from which God is banished. The list could go on and on.[3]

The result is the dechristianization of behaviour, not only in the wider culture but among Christian people as well. There may be a renewal of interest in the gospel in North America, but is there a renewal of Christian behaviour? We hope that will come, but in the meantime to be realistic must we not admit that we are compromising our standards and losing our distinctives? We may chuckle at the Amish who refuse to send their children to statist schools and at fundamentalists who refuse to drink or smoke or attend movies. But what right have we got to laugh at them? They understood that there was a war on between Christianity and the world — it is unclear that we understand that these days. We face the possible loss of the Christian way of life today.

Let us take some examples of concern. The breakup of the family has reached crisis proportions. Christian families hardly seem more stable than others in this regard. We find some evangelicals even coming out in support of homosexual behaviour and abortion on demand in the name of civil rights. We stand in danger of losing the Christian family which is the primary focus of Christian education and nurture. Sexual morality is another area of great concern. In recent decades we have seen the growing acceptance of common law marriages, sex before marriage, exotic forms of intercourse, and general promiscuity. Herpes and Aids disease are probably more influential in stemming this tide of immorality than Christian teaching. In the name of freedom and self-actualization we are becoming decadent. In the area of entertainment we are seeing pornography coming into every home with a VCR or pay-TV and more and more degrading language and actions of violence and exploitation. And what do we make of rock music like the Rolling Stones and Black Sabbath? or the flood of sex magazines in every corner milk store? Is there any difference between Christians and non-Christians in the kind of entertainment they enjoy?

Finally, let me mention the power of possessions in the affluent West. Christians are using their new wealth for the most part not to advance the kingdom, but to make their own lives more comfortable. How else can we explain the summer cottages, the recreational vehicles, the home computers, the vacations overseas, the new cars, the larger homes, the dishwashers? Yes, there is a lot of generosity too — toward local church, community charities, and world mission and relief. But on the whole we have a lot of affluent Christians who spend their money on themselves and give the extra to good causes. They do not cut into the North American way of life to advance the kingdom of God even though the needs are urgent.

Is there any evidence that Christians handle their possessions differently than non-believers do? We face a crisis of individual

Christian behaviour. We are rapidly being assimilated into worldly patterns without seeming to be aware of it. No wonder Paul speaks of 'the wiles of the Devil' (Eph 6:11). We must begin to take seriously the task of applying Christian standards of behaviour to the new situation we face. Obviously this will mean strengthening the family and the church as the primary groupings in which we can preserve and pass along Christian ways of behaving. Furthermore it will mean making available solid teaching and counsel in regard to Christian living, in the home, on the job, and at school. By all means let us remember that in the confrontation between Christianity and secular modernity the Christian way of life as well as the Christian confession of faith is at stake. We are called to believe and to behave according to the Word of God.

Mobilizing Our Corporate Lifestyle

The Bible also challenges us to restore the creation and reclaim the culture for God and the gospel. This mandate presents certain challenges to our understanding as well as to our acting. Therefore I will spend a little more time on it. Basically there are two problems we need to discuss before setting forth an agenda for Christian action in North America. Both involve mistakes that need to be corrected.

The first is the problem of so-called privatized religion. For a number of reasons which can be identified, conservative Christians in North America have been until recently ineffective as a cultural force. They have held forth the gospel of personal experience, but they have not pursued the creation mandate to take dominion. Even though our evangelical forbears like Calvin, Wesley, Booth and Wilberforce managed to combine belief in the everlasting gospel with a healthy degree of social concern, somehow their descendants have forgotten how to do so. Why is this? One reason is surely eschatology. People have been taught that there is no point polishing the brass on a sinking ship, that is, they have been told to believe that the world is getting worse and worse till the coming of the Lord, and have concluded quite intelligently that there is not much use trying to reform society. That have imbibed an eschatology of defeat instead of an eschatology of victory. Add to that the fact that the liberals do very little else besides social action, and the recipe for uninvolvement is almost complete. After all, who wants any part in a liberal program for reconstruction of society, especially when it sounds vaguely like bringing the socialists to power? So it has happened that large numbers of conservative Christians until recently have not swung their weight behind the reclamation of the culture.[4]

Fortunately this is quickly changing. There are signs everywhere that evangelical Christians are beginning to be disturbed enough at what is happening to do something. The liberal left calls it predictably the resurgence of the 'new right,' but what it is properly speaking is a true revival of Christian social concerns. You see it in the founding of thousands of Christian schools, in the groundswell of opposition to the scandal of abortion, in the backlash against the gay and feminist crusades, in the opposition to the propoganda of evolution in the schools, in the reaction against big messianic government, in the opposition to totalitarianism in the world, in the insistence that crime be punished, and so on and on. It is not ideologically right wing in essence, but rather a new desire to express our Christian faith in the public arena and to return to traditional Christian values. Thus, while the privatization of religion is a problem in North American Christianity, it is rapidly ceasing to be the problem it once was.

There is a problem of ideology in contemporary Christian social ethics, but it lies more on the left than on the right. Just as we face a basically false gospel in the area of liberal theology (chapter one), so we face a basically deluded praxis in the area of liberal social ethics. Because so many people are being taken in by it, let me expose the nature of this ideological praxis here.[5] It is surely a wonderful piece of irony that now that privatism is passing we should be faced with a radical alternative which is hardly preferable to what it is replacing. One thing at least you can say for socially uninvolved conservatives — they never supported Stalin or marched on behalf of Pol Pot! When one looks at the astonishing set of fallacies set forth by left-wing social ethics today, it is a serious question whether it is better than privatized religion.

To get at this hydra-headed monster the easiest route for me to take is my own recent experience as the point of departure. The decade of the 60's was a heady time to grow up in North America. It was a time for utopian idealism, when we dreamed about equality and fraternity, and delighted to hate the world of democratic capitalism. We extolled the virtues of a social order which did not exist anywhere, and savagely criticized the only society we knew. We could hardly wait for the overthrow of America for its exploitation, and the dawning of the paradise which would surely follow. Once we had restored the means of production to the people there would be no poverty or racism or injustice. Amerika (for so we spelled it) was doomed but the horizon was bright with the promise of a new day. In retrospect I suppose we hated ourselves for the crime of being born into affluent homes but did not realize it at the time.

Politically we were socialists if anything. We loved to repeat the shrill left-wing critique of capitalism. Nothing was too severe to say. We hated the banks, the multinationals, the liberals, the military-industrial complex. And we loved the third world and its socialist experiments. How joyful we became recounting the triumphs of the Tanzanian or Chinese or Cuban people who had succeeded in overthrowing the yoke placed upon them by American imperialism. It was all so exciting and it all rang so true. We even founded a paper, now called *Sojourners*, where all these things could be printed and distributed. It felt good to be alive.[6]

The same kind of radical causes were being espoused at the same time by the World Council of Churches and by the various national councils of churches. Some of the commonplace causes can easily be listed: the unilateral disarmament of the West, support for Marxist guerillas wherever they were working, support for the PLO terrorist organization, a concern for human rights so long as they were abused in non-communist settings, incessant railings against the United States, a whitewashing of the Soviet Union and what it was doing, opposition to industrial development, silence about the persecution of Jews and Christians in Russia, opposition to any attempt to resist murderous regimes being put in place in South East Asia, ridicule toward the freedoms of the West, and so on and on.[7]

It would not have been so bad if we had just put forward these doubtful propositions as opinions of ours which they were. After all, in a free country one may hold to his opinions even if they threaten the very freedom which makes them possible were they ever implemented. But, no, we went on and sanctified our revolutionary opinions. We said that it had something to do with God's kingdom to believe in them. Mao Tse Tung type revolutionaries had some role to play in the dawning of a new humanity. This had two effects: first it removed the doubt which would inevitably have arisen had the opinions been considered on their actual merit, and second it made it possible for really foolish notions to enjoy a longer life than they otherwise would have. Who else today lives in the intellectual world of the 60's but the churchmen?

Fortunately I can report to have awoken from this bad dream

along with a good number of other inhabitants of the 80's. Reality can often break through our dreaming innocence and restore us to consciousness. First of all the cultural alienation began to disappear. I started to notice the value and importance in the West of such practices as free speech, limited government, an independent judiciary, an unharassed church, genuine pluralism, and a concern for human rights, including dubious rights — the very things which are so noticeably lacking in most of the rest of the world and for which the West shines like a beacon of hope to the nations even today. I look back and wonder how I could have been so blind to be so contemptuous of a society which gave me so much of what was decent, human, and really Christian. How could I have been attracted to those socialist experiments which turn out time and again to be hopeless failures and often death camps as well? Why in looking for signs of the kingdom (a very proper thing to do) did I consistently look in the wrong places? Whatever the answer is, it gradually dawned upon me that I had been viewing the world wrongly, and that if one must label a society 'babylonian' there are many more worthy candidates for that honour than North American society. This is not to deny that there are flaws in Western culture which pain me as a Christian, or that I no longer feel deep concern for the wretched of the earth. In that department nothing has changed. What is different is that I now see that the West embodies values which are uniquely precious at this juncture in history and must not be lost sight of.[9]

Politically speaking, I have come to realize what I should have known all along that North American society is a sign of hope in the world for whatever freedom, prosperity, peace and justice we may hope to have, while the socialist block is largely a zone of crushed hopes and deceitful propaganda. It is simply astonishing to consider the folly of Western intellectuals and churchmen over the past half century for the way in which they have been drawn to support one oppressive regime after another simply because it told them the lies they wanted to hear.[10] The failure to see the deadly implications of the totalitarian menace in the 20th century, from Hitler to Stalin, and all their mad successors, constitutes a devastating judgment on Western intellectual leaders.[11] How could we have been so blind not to see that the flaws of our own society were incomparably small when compared with the butchery practised by world communism in the name of humanity.[12] I am talking about a deep sickness among us which, if it succeeds in bringing down the West which it is committed to do, will introduce a period in world history ten times more miserable than our present experience. The West is a far cry from the kingdom of God, but if we are looking for signs of hope where else shall we find them?

In terms of economics I have come to believe that the left is suffering from cruel delusions, delusions which foster totalitarianism. Surely one of the most obvious lessons recent experience has taught us is that government planning in the economy is a monumental failure while market economics has the proven ability to produce wealth for the people. Individual economic agents are in a better position to judge what actions to take than the government which cannot possibly take account of the vast flow of information which the market handles. All countries with centrally planned economies have failed and are failing, while economic growth is only being experienced in situations where economic freedom is tolerated. Ironically there are far more people able to rationalize the failure of socialism than there are people able to explain why the market succeeds so well. For this reason the market system which offers so much hope economically is seriously threatened today. The goose that lays the golden eggs is about to be slaughtered by the intellectuals so well paid and sustained by its products.[13]

All one needs to do to see the truth of this is to consider the case of India and compare it to Japan and Hong Kong. India has enormously greater resources of land and claims on foreign aid. But India has remained relatively stagnant economically while Japan and Hong Kong have rushed ahead. While cultural factors play a role, the answer cannot be that Indians as such are unproductive because when they have emigrated very often they have prospered and invigorated the places where they have settled. No, the simple and correct answer is that Japan has gone ahead because it relies primarily on the engine of the free market while India is stagnant because it has adopted the model of central economic planning. They have followed the Russian pattern of five year plans and created a sluggish system which penalizes creativity and ambition. The comparison between India and Japan and even more so Hong Kong vividly proves the folly of Christian theology sanctifying an economy of controls rather than an economy of freedom.[14]

Far from being willing to see this, these ideological theologians pin the blame on the West for poverty in places like India. They listen to demagogues like Julius Nyerere of Tanzania who heap blame upon capitalism while covering up their own colossal follies.

It is estimated that his country has received more in foreign aid than it raises itself in taxes and export earnings. All the while the government uses this money to collectivize agriculture and suppress private economic activity with devastating results on production and distribution. Thousands have been uprooted from their homes and famine stalks the land, while Western churchmen hold Nyerere up as a saint and prophetic voice from the third world. If this be prophecy, it is false prophecy. Far from being the cause of third world poverty, the West has been the principal agent of material progress there. The kind of centrally planned dictatorships the trendy left-wing clerics have been supporting for decades are the worst enemy of any advancement in the material fortunes of poor people in those countries. State control in the economy results in an inefficient allocation of resources and therefore deepens poverty and does nothing to relieve it.[15]

This was all made tolerably clear to me when I visited Mexico to attend a conference of liberation theologians there in 1983. I was told that poverty in Latin America was the result of the rapacious economy of North America and that I ought to go back to Canada and work for change of a socialist kind. But I had to ask myself if this was true. Here was Mexico with huge land holdings, a favorable climate, oil reserves, and a solid population. Yet Mexico was up to its ears in debt and full of people trying to get out across the United States border. Where did all these resources go which were given by the banks and gushed from the ground? Why was poverty a problem here? Cultural factors aside, there was only one real explanation. Mexico has opted for an economy which is dominated by the state, and the results have been disastrous. Whatever injustices there may be in the relationship between Mexico and America can certainly not begin to account for the problems of this economy which must be laid squarely on the lap of foolish economic policy. You reap what you sow, and not only in spiritual matters.[16]

Canada is in much better shape than Mexico because state intervention in the economy has not gone quite so far. Nevertheless, we have a huge budget deficit, larger proportionately than the United States, and not the result of defense expenditures in which we are in fact derelict in our duty to NATO. The Canadian dollar is sagging around 77c US and our inflation is higher than in the United States. The government has nationalized hundreds of what it likes to call 'crown corporations' many of which are losing money hand over fist and for which public accounting is seldom available. We have had a national energy policy which has practically destroyed the oil industry and marketing boards for all kinds of products which distort supply and demand and maintain unnecessarily high prices. Unemployment is high and government policies discourage capital formation and investment, including foreign investment in Canada as if it were an act of imperialism.

We also have a group of Catholic bishops who like to reflect ethically on the economy and to propose solutions for the problems. Their themes echo the left-wing line and touch upon greater redistribution of wealth, less technological advancement, increased government intervention in and control of the market, and larger powers to labour unions.[17] Although I admire the concern shown by the bishops, their ideas of what would help the situation are almost entirely fallacious.[18] The effect of following their suggestions would almost certainly make the situation much worse by carrying us still deeper into the morass of federal government economic planning which has already brought the country almost to its knees. Questions with devastating implications have to be asked: how can wealth be redistributed if it is not being produced? why move to wage and price controls which only create a host of new problems? with ever higher levels of welfare, what incentive is there for accepting an entry position job in the economy? why give the government more authority to intervene in the market when its interventions of late have been failing so dismally? why give greater power to unions who only seek higher wages for their own members regardless of productivity? why is deficit budgeting unimportant when it fuels inflation which hurts the poor most? is not opposing technical innovations something like objecting to the invention of the wheel?[19]

With the kind of ideological social ethics I have been discussing, Christians are squandering what little credibility they have left in the modern world, and saying nothing of any positive value towards alleviating the problems of our time. First, we must cease discrediting the gospel by prostituting it to the interests of the political left, and second, we must come up with an agenda for our society which is scriptural and intelligent.

Fortunately since I penned these words the Canadian people have thrown out of office the liberal government of Pierre Trudeau and returned the Progressive Conservatives under Brian Mulroney to power. The size of their victory strongly suggests that we will now be moving ahead with policies which favour the power of the market to produce wealth and welfare, and away from those which imprison Canadians in a morass of government regulation, waste, and inefficiency.

Claiming our Nation for God

What then ought we to be doing in response to the call of the kingdom and in a contextual way to further the work of God in Canada? What can we say that would not be ideologically captive either to the left or to the right? How can we move, not only toward a spiritual renewal in the churches, but also toward the political renovation of our country?

i. First of all Christians must pray for their government and for all who are in high positions, that we may lead a quiet and peaceable life, godly and respectful in every way" (1 Tim 2:2). Without in any way making an idol out of our nation, or refusing to criticize it when it goes astray, we ought to be enormously thankful to God for a country which gives liberty to the Christian faith. The 20th century has been the dreadful era of huge gangster states such as Nazi Germany and the Soviet Union which have seized all power for themselves and murdered those who object. We ought to be very thankful to God that we live in a political order where the power is not concentrated in only one institution but is distributed among many. The church, the family, and the economy all enjoy a degree of liberty from the encroaching state. This means that we live in a country where it is possible to operate in our Christian mission without opposition and to criticize the political order without fear of reprisal. What has made this possible is precisely democratic capitalism. Far from perfect, this polity has allowed the greatest measure of human freedom ever experienced in history.[20] Freedom is snuffed out when power is concentrated in one institution — it is created when the power is shared among many institutions. Thus it is not ideologically right wing to say we ought to support democratic capitalism. It is simply that we support those conditions which make it possible to be Christians without resistance or persecution. Judged by the one-way traffic of refugees in the world today toward the West, I would say that a lot more people than Christians long for this liberty.[21] Christians benefit from the liberty given in a liberal society — therefore, we support democratic capitalism.

ii. Since we live in a society which permits it, we ought to seek to christianize the social order. This would be part of our mission whether or not our country had strongly Christian roots or a Christian majority among its citizens. The fact that it has both only makes this imperative all the more obvious and legitimate. Canada is not basically Muslim or Hindu or even Jewish — it is basically Christian, despite immigration policies designed to change that fact. Therefore, we will seek to make the society reflect its Christian character. Our laws ought not to reflect the minority opinion of secular humanism as they are now tending to do, but reflect Christian values. It was the influence of the Christian faith which led to Western society and its liberty and prosperity. And we must continue to insist that our nation be governed according to biblical truth. We are not a humanist country which knows no divine standards of right and wrong and operates in the vacuum of moral relativism. We are a nation under God, a nation which belongs to Jesus Christ, and a nation whose Christian foundations we must pledge to refurbish. A battle needs to be fought against the forces of secularism which want to bring Canada down to ruin by policies of statism and godlessness. Jesus Christ did not come only to save souls from hell. He came to claim the creation he himself made and to establish his rule over all peoples. Therefore the state as well as the church ought to be ruled by God's law so that righteousness may exalt our nation. Let us therefore gather all our forces and stand up for righteousness in our society and bring our country back to moral sanity. Let us join hands with our brothers and sisters south of the border who have gone further in this direction than we have, and bring North America back to God and God's Word.

There never was a golden age when North America was ideally Christian nor do I expect one in the near future. But it does strain historical memory to recall a time less than a century ago when there was a solid Christian consensus in our culture. It was a time when we would not have had to see brutalization in the media or the slaughter of the unborn in our hospitals or a massive state creeping into every corner of our lives. There was a humaneness to the public square which derived from the Christian religion. There were basic moral values which marked our society off as Judeo-Christian. And we have seen the erosion and loss of this treasure. Christians worthy of their salt ought to be committed to recovering it.

This does not imply a Christian theocracy on the order of the Islamic republic in Iran. We are neither utopians who intend to force feed the population on unwanted morals, nor bigots who do not allow for genuine differences of opinion. Quite the contrary, religious tolerance and political pluralism are two of the great gifts to us of the modern era including the Reformation. People who burn the books of others can expect to have their own books burned next. By all means we want to allow for debate and discussion on matters of public polity and morality. But at the same time there were basic moral values which informed our culture in the past and made it great, moral values which we must now be committed to see returned to prominence. Canada under the greater influence of God's Word will be a better and more humane place to live than it is today.

iii. In terms of social issues our most pressing concern must be to protect the health and vitality of the family. Along with church and state, the family is one of the three most important arrangements established by God to govern human affairs. It is a fundamental building block of society and the basic instrument of Christian nurture, and yet it is under fantastic pressure and attack today. Marital fidelity is being swept away in a flood of sexual promiscuity, and families are breaking up by the thousands. Unborn babies are being slaughtered, and children are being secularized in the public schools. It is time to take a stand.

Supporting the family involves us in a cluster of issues. One of them is sexually permissive morality which eats away at the fidelity a sound family presupposes. In the name of self-fulfilment people today are justifying fornication, homosexuality, and pornography which will bring our society down to ruin. We oppose such things not because they are sexual, but because they are the enemy of true sexuality as God created it. They degrade human beings, especially women, and they eat away at the social fabric. We must vocally oppose pornography, abortion mills, no-fault divorce, and homosexuality in order to strengthen at least a basic level of morality in our nation.

This opens up a number of related issues. We have to stand against the pornography explosion. *Playboy* is now very conservative, sticking pretty much to straight heterosexual exploitation. But what about child pornography? "Sex before eight or it's too late." What about handbooks explaining how to seduce children? We are dealing here with a crime which is leading our nation into decadence and to the judgment that it deserves from Almighty God. This is no time to say pornography is not so important in light of other concerns. Let us make our voice heard on this crucial matter.

And what about abortion? Although God declares human life to be precious, millions of unborn babies are being terminated by medical violence because they are inconvenient lives. What kind of civilization is it which performs atrocities on such a scale? Today we kill the unborn children, tomorrow it will be the elderly and the incurably ill and the insane. Hitler will have won his war upon the West posthumously.[22]

Abortion is not the only immorality now being cloaked under the name of human rights. Homosexuality and radical feminism also seek to win acceptance in society by legal changes. So-called gays are trying to make it illegal for any employer to take homosexuality into account in his hiring practices. An effort is being made to have homosexuality accepted as an alternative lifestyle, as valid in its own way as heterosexuality. But according to the Bible it is not. It is in fact one of many marks of moral decadence (Rom 1:24-25). It is not worse than a number of other deviancies, but it is a threat to a morally sound society and will lead us if unchecked into ruin. Christians care about gay people, but do not recognize any right to an acceptable lifestyle for homosexuality. It is a warped condition, and a corrupting practice which must be resisted.

Radical feminism is a threat to society also but in a more subtle way. The idea that males and females are the same and have no physiological differences which make it proper to make distinctions in their social roles is not only dreaming but also potentially harmful to the family and to women and men. Christians ought to support economic justice and equal opportunity for women, but not policies which would discriminate against women who have chosen the traditional role of mother and homemaker. Radical feminists despise the biblical and traditional family which is a patriarchal polity, and are determined to overthrow it. We must not let them.

Public education has become a crucial family issue too. Although Canada preserves a religious dimension in the public schools which contrasts favorably with the situation in the United States, it is still increasingly true that the ethos in public education is secularist. Even though God entrusted children to parents and commanded them to raise them in the fear and knowledge of God, we Christian parents still send our offspring to public schools where they try to learn without any reference to God or the relevance of divine revelation to the subjects of education. Teachers and textbooks very often inculcate a humanist orientation and secularize Christian young people. We had better make up our minds. Either to protest the godlessness of the public schools or to abandon them and form Christian schools where God is honored and his Word heard. We have delayed long enough — it is time to act.

iv. In terms of political issues the most pressing concern is to limit the powers of the state and call upon government to do what God established it to do.

Let me deal first with the economy and the need to roll back state intervention in it. A liberation of the economy is in order if we hope to release our wealth-producing capacity and meet the needs of the poor.

Governments were set up in order to bring the lawless to justice and to protect the citizens from their enemies within and without. But in Canada the government is so busy sticking its nose into the economy and messing it up it fails in its primary duty.

The picture of state intervention in the economy is a mixture of follies and injustices. The basic injustices are three: the deficit, theft by taxation, and the inflation of the money supply. Because of irresponsible spending, the politicians of North America have run up a huge public debt which will burden all future budgets because of crippling interest payments which will rob future generations. Christians must see this, not only as foolish policy, but in moral terms, as theft. Spending money that has not been collected is immoral and ought to be made illegal. Increases in the money supply which causes inflation is also theft. Greedy to create larger revenues, the government prints more paper money to relieve its financial embarrassment. Instead of raising taxes and risking voter wrath, it orders an increase in the money supply and pays some of its bills out of that. It looks like they are getting extra money for nothing, but in actual fact they are simply diluting the value of all money in circulation and forcing prices up. It is a hidden way of taxing all the money out there. In a word, it is debauching the currency. It is mixing lead with silver. It is doing what God forbids in his law, and which the prophets railed against. Theft also shows up in the system of progressive taxation. Instead of everyone paying a flat rate, productive people pay more than others. They pay more taxes because they bettered themselves and earned a higher income. Although we have gotten used to the practice, Christians can only speak of it in moral terms as an expropriation of property by a greedy government. People may wish to defend the policy of taking from the rich and giving to the poor by the state, but the moral reality is unaffected: socialism is theft. What else can we call the forcible seizure of people's goods and their redistribution to others? Thus, our primary objection to Canadian politics as it bears upon the economy is that it is unjust government.

Even more obvious to even more people are the follies being perpetrated under the pretense of a centrally planned economy. Wherever the state endeavours to control in detail the economic activities of its citizens, the people find their living standard lowered, their freedom jeopardized, and prosperity flowing in only one direction toward the aggrandisement of the state itself. As regards the state, the saying is true 'small is beautiful'. Excessive government as we have it in Canada imposes high costs upon our resources, impedes growth, and produces giant inefficiencies. It is urgent that we bring it into line. Everywhere in the world, oil prices are going down, but not in Canada. Why? Because government, seeking a pot of gold, got into the energy business and cooked up a deal to raise prices. The state acquired its own oil company, and regulated the rest of the industry, with the result that oil exploration practically ceased and we are all paying absurdly high prices for petroleum. In all this there is little of seeing Canada self-sufficient in energy in this century. Canada is the prisoner of government economic policies which have failed and with no hope in sight.[23]

But organizations like Petro-Canada are but a drop in the bucket. The federal government alone, not to mention what provincial governments own, has control of at least two hundred 'crown corporations' (a euphemistic term for nationalized industries). In this way the state is lurching into the market place to compete with private investment. Every day the news is filled with fresh reports of new losses in these corporations, despite efforts of the government to prevent the public finding out such facts. Christians must insist on public disclosure in relation to these acquisitions, and urge the gradual withdrawal of government from all such areas.

The list of follies goes on and on. Government in Canada is sapping the vitality of our country. First, there is the minimum wage law which throws thousands of people out of work. It requires employers to pay workers at least $4 an hour or more in some provinces even if their productivity rates fall below that figure. This guarantees unemployment to those who need it most. Second, Canada imposes tariffs upon goods entering the country which means that consumers are prevented from purchasing the best product at the lowest price. Again, it is the poor most affected. Third, excessive government regulation of the economy means that thousands are unemployed because freedom and creativity are squelched. For example, one could not enter the taxi cab market if he wanted to. Fourth, price controls are imposed on products such as eggs and milk which sets the price artificially high, again robbing the poor. Fifth, we have a cradle to the grave welfare system which creates a huge class of dependant people and makes even businessmen line up to receive government handouts. Aside from the inevitable unfairness of the dole, even governments with their power of printing paper money have been having trouble paying the tab and the quality of life is actually sinking under the system. Instead of creating self-reliant individuals, we are producing wards of the state and at the same time bankrupting ourselves.

Most of these policies are promoted paternalistically. If we wise politicians do not care for the needy, who will? And behind it lies the shrewd political sense, we can keep getting the votes if we hand out other people's money. Christians need to be saying that the hope of the poor does not lie with bloated statism. The welfare and socialist state is the enemy of the poor. It socializes nothing but poverty itself. If we care about the poor, if we want to exercise 'the preferential option for the poor' which the liberationists talk about, then we would discard the foolish policies of this kind and adopt market economics. It may be the worst system in some eyes — it just happens to be better than any other!

What is the hope for the poor of the world? In part it is the generosity of God's people who respond to the cries of the needy and share what they have with them. But that is not the real answer over the long haul. We could divest ourselves of everything we own and not put a dint in the real problem of the poor, because the problem of the poor is unproductivity. Wealth is produced through productivity and capital investment. The reason the average American is wealthier and able to consume more than the average Indian or Chinese is simple: production per head in India and China is many times lower than it is in America. Wealth comes from long practised habits of industry and capital formation. If a culture cannot or will not act this way, due to its religion or politics, it will be poor, and has no one to blame but itself. Accepting for a moment the myth of a 'third world', unless there is a positive attitude to material advancement and a sense of personal responsibility among the people, there is no way that poverty can be overcome. Tanzanians may wish to believe the lie that the West is to blame for their plight, but that will not change the truth one iota. Unless they adopt material productive attitudes and permit individual economic agents to operate in an atmosphere of freedom, they are doomed to be poor perpetually. To be full of envy and to believe lies may feel good, but the only hope for the relief of poverty in the world is capital accumulation and productivity, which means, cultural obedience to God's law for human affairs.

Thus there are biblical economic principles involved in this issue. The state has little to do with it. Its task is to protect the citizens from criminals and invading enemies. God has given the earth to our dominion. People have the right to own property on it and the responsibility to manage their possessions in a righteous and godly way. Prosperity and material advancement comes through diligent labour and wise planning. There is nothing surprising about the wealth of the West. It is the direct outgrowth of the Puritan ethic of diligent labour and investment. It flows to those who perform best according to God's order of dominion through service. In this way God gives power to get wealth, and requires that people act ethically in the process of exchange and interaction. No one should claim that the Bible teaches capitalist economics *per se*. But it does set forth those principles which are consistent with a free and non-statist economy, and are violated in so much socialist theory and practice.

The Bible also promises long term blessings of both worldwide peace and economic abundance to those who heed God's law. God will be exalted in all the earth and all nations will be blessed in him. As this begins to come about I believe we will see material blessings flowing to the godly and capital shifting from unproductive armaments to beneficial endeavours. Not through acts of humanistic statism, but through the power of the gospel of Jesus Christ. One day the heritage of the heathen will belong to Christ, and then truly there will be no more poor among us.

v. As we are calling on the state to desist from trying to do what it cannot and should not do in the economic sector, Christians must be calling upon government to do what it can and ought to do. The proper role of the state according to the Bible is very simple — to bring wrongdoers to justice and punish them (Rom 13:1-7). When you have said that, you have said just about everything. But the irony today is that the modern state is failing even at this. Let me comment briefly on the two main areas, criminal justice and defense.

Crime is a frightening problem in North America. Yet the offenders have been given far more rights than society and the victims of their crimes. The answer is surely not more prisons, but more restitution. Biblical law says nothing about prisons, but says a lot about the moral responsibility of wrongdoers to pay back and make good the harm they have done. Furthermore it prescribes the death penalty for a number of offenses which pollute the earth for their ugliness. Christians today must take a strong stand for restitution instead of prisons, and the immediate restoration of the death penalty. Imagine a mass murderer who ought to die according to God's just law, living on in a 'corrections' facility at the cost to taxpayers of over a half a million dollars, and then go free after 25 years!

Protecting the nation is a basic government responsibility which concerns the very existence of the nation. Until the election of Reagan in the United States and leaders such as Mitterand and Thatcher in other countries, commitment to the defense of the West had been slipping badly and the Soviet Union had been allowed to overtake us in military preparedness. How ironical that so many so-called Christians should be lending their support for a 'peace movement' which is little more than a front for the Soviet aim for the takeover of the free world! We in Canada have a more shameful record than most. While our last prime minister Trudeau is trotting around the world 'seeking peace', our military forces are shamefully weak and ill-equipped and our commitments to NATO unfulfilled. Yet we criticize the Americans for rearming in the face of a terrifying Soviet buildup. Let Christians speak to the hypocrisy of Canada, and to the negligence of her federal government.[24]

Is this a right wing agenda then? No it is not. Christians ought to stand for a liberal society which celebrates freedom in its midst. The left and the right, facism and socialism, are both statist and totalitarian in tendency. What we must call for in Canada, is a limited state, and a free society in which people can live out their commitment or noncommitment to the Lord. We are not uncritical of the West. We do not identify North America with the kingdom of God. We do not equate our enemies with God's enemies. We bow to no ideology at all. We give allegiance to God and his law.

A Plan of Action

First, we have to be serious about teaching people biblical principles and disciple them to carry them out. Sunday Schools are boring today because we have lost the vision of what we are supposed to train people to do. So we fill up the time with unfruitful study. Once we wake up to the fact that our job is to reclaim the creation and the culture for God, our agenda will start to fill up with meaningful items. Second, we have to start being vocal about specific issues. There are plenty to choose from: abortion, pornography, deficits, educational brainwashing, and the like. Let us begin to resist what is going on, and make a difference by laying our bodies down. Third, we should tie evangelism to the social mandate. When we preach Christ, we are not just offering a happiness pill and hell-fire insurance, we are asking people to join in the dominion mandate and come aboard the kingdom train. Evangelism needs to be issues oriented. Perhaps we should start a Christian school to stem the tide of secular humanism. Maybe we should organize the neighbourhood working with the police to ensure the protection of property. Maybe a counselling service is what is desperately needed. Door to door witnessing is rather fruitless — bread and butter evangelism is more promising and more to the point. Fourth, let us elect godly politicans who support biblical principles and get rid of the humanists who are in politics for power and money and are tearing our country apart. Hopefully by the time this book is published the political scene will have become more promising.

Let us put an end to our wishywashyness. We have been quiet and docile long enough, watching the secularists take the culture away from us. We have a message and we have the outlines of a program. Let us get down to work and move Canada in the direction of a Christian commonwealth.

Questions for Discussion

1.Why do Christians sometimes have trouble seeing the dominion mandate of the Bible?
2. Do you think the ideological social action of the liberals has kept evangelicals from moving ahead in this area?
3. What local issues could your church latch on to in order to do issues oriented evangelism?

For Further Reading

John J. Davis, *Your Wealth in God's World. Does the Bible Support the Free Market?* (Presbyterian and Reformed, 1984)

Ronald H. Nash, *Social Justice and the Christian Church.* (Mott Media, 1983)

Mark A. Noll, Nathan O. Hatch, and George M. Marsden, *The Search for Christian America.* (Crossway Books, 1983)

Francis A.Schaeffer, *A Christian Manifesto.* (Crossway Books, 1981)

Conclusion

Like Nehemiah we face a miserable situation in the churches. There is widespread doctrinal declension. Whereas heresy used to plague the church from the outside, nowadays it saps her strength from within as well. In addition we face spiritual lukewarmness and cultural ineffectiveness. Like Nehemiah we ought to weep. "When I (Nehemiah) heard these words I sat down and wept, and mourned for days, and I continued fasting and praying before the God of heaven" (Neh 1:4). But Nehemiah did not stop with praying, he heard God's call to go to Jerusalem and rebuild her walls (2:5, 17-18). He decided to take action, and we must do the same.

First, we have to return to the apostolic and biblical truth foundations. The gospel is in great danger from false teaching, and we must guard it. The Christian faith is being threatened by an increasingly radical and basically humanistic theology of the left. The church is being tempted to accommodate her confession and her lifestyle to the world's patterns. A growing church conflict, not dissimilar to the one in Nazi Germany, is spreading like a cancer across all denominations, and it concerns the ability of the church to speak a true Word of God. Nothing less than the integrity of the gospel is at stake. Teachers in the churches are spreading opinions which in earlier times would have correctly been viewed as heresies. Salvation through the finished work and glorious resurrection of the incarnate Son of God is the message we stand to lose if action is not taken.[1] The call goes out to us as well as to Timothy: "Preach the Word" (2 Tim 2:2).

Second, we must open ourselves without reservation to the power of the outpoured Spirit. A church like Sardis cannot accomplish the work of God: "you have the name of being alive, and you are dead" (Rev 3:2). A church like Laodicea cannot please God: "because you are lukewarm, and neither cold nor hot, I will spew you out of my mouth" (Rev 3:16). We must turn to God in repentance and ask him to restore to us the spiritual vitality we used to know. In my spirit I believe God wants us to hear his promise in words addressed to Israel:

> On that day I will cleanse you from all your iniquities, I will cause the cities to be inhabited, and the waste places shall be rebuilt. And the land that was desolate shall be tilled, instead of being the desolation that it was in the sight of all who passed by. And they will say, "This land that was desolate has become like the garden of Eden, and the waste and desolate and ruined cities are now inhabited and fortified." Then the nations that are left round about you shall know that I, the Lord, have rebuilt the ruined places, and replanted that which was desolate. I, the Lord, have spoken, and I will do it. (Ezek 36: 33-36)

Third, we must be willing to follow the Lord in costly discipleship and give heed to his law. The forces of darkness have gathered to oppose the gospel and the work of God. Like Goliath of old they are defying the armies of the people of God (1 Sam 17:10). Will a David arise in our generation to say in effect: "Who is this uncircumcised Philistine that he should defy the armies of the living God? The Lord who delivered me from the paw of the lion and from the paw of the bear, will deliver me from the hand of this Philistine" (1 Sam 17:26, 37). Ungodliness and injustice stalk our land. Let us call for and spearhead a return to scriptural values in personal and public morality. Let us not permit false ideological politics of the left to blind us to our God-given mission. "Righteousness exalts a nation" — therefore, let us move in the direction of Christian reconstruction.

If we take a stand in these areas, I believe that God will bless the churches of our land. But taking a stand will not be easy. As soon as Nehemiah set out to restore Jerusalem, he faced opposition from those who hated the reformation he had in mind. They attacked him physically and morally; they taunted and slandered him; they lied and ridiculed him (Neh 2:10, 18; 4:1; 6:2, 6). We cannot expect any civility from the liberals when we go after the heart of their apostate theology. We should not expect a host of nominal Christians in our pews to welcome the stirrings of a revival. We ought not to be surprised when the chorus of ridicule comes in response to our plans to rechristianize Canada.

But opposition did not deter Nehemiah from obeying the will of God, and it did not prevent him from winning the battle. God frustrated the plans of his enemies, and the walls of Jerusalem were rebuilt in spite of them (Neh 4:15; 6:15). And so it shall be with us in Canada. I believe that if we take a strong stand in the areas indicated God will pour out a blessing upon us there will not be room enough to receive. Remember that Nehemiah was empowered because he remembered the promise of God: "If you return to me, and keep my commandments, and do them, though your dispersed be under the farthest sky, I will gather them thence and bring them to the place which I have chosen, to make my name dwell there" (Neh 1:9).

You see, we are not playing games. There is a God who has given his Word and made rich promises, and what I am speaking about in this book we can count upon God to bless if we do it. We lift up God's truth, God's Spirit, and God's law — and not the word and ability of man. God is waiting to bless and to perform his Word among us.

Moses speaks to us today: "I have set before you this day life and good, death and evil. If you obey the commandments of the Lord, by loving the Lord your God, by walking in his ways, and by keeping his commandments and his statutes and his ordinances, then you shall live . . . but if your heart turns away, and you will not hear, but are drawn away to worship other gods and serve them, I declare to you this day, that you shall perish" (Deut 30:15-18). Moses set before the people a great choice between life and death, blessing and cursing, and urged them to choose life. I am making the same appeal now. I have a vision in my heart of a great and renewed biblical Christian movement in Canada, purified in its doctrine, revitalized in its life, and zealous for social change. As the hymn says, 'mercy drops around us are falling, but for the showers we plead.'

Can we be optimistic about the future? Can we hope for a renaissance of conservative Christianity in Canada? Yes, I think we can. Not only because it is already happening as we can see from the patterns of church attendance and in statistics relating to theological education and missionary activity. But more importantly because Jesus Christ is on the throne. We do not serve a defeated Christ, but the Lord of heaven and earth with all power at his disposal. We can have ascension eyes through which to see his victory coming to pass in our land. Too long we have been content to be ineffectual and number two. For too long we have been like the ten spies who drew back from wanting to enter the promised land because of fear. From now on let us be like Joshua and Caleb who believed in the promise and in the power of God, and knew that God's kingdom could not be stopped by any foe. Jesus Christ is Lord. Satan has been defeated.

All Christ's enemies are going to be placed beneath his feet. He will reign forever and ever, and we will reign with him. There is no room for pessimism or long faces here. Minor setbacks we may experience, but defeat? Never. Jesus Christ is Lord and he will have dominion 'from sea to sea and from the river to the ends of the earth' (Psalm 72:8). The future is neither blocked or even uncertain. The leaven will leaven the whole lump — it is only a matter of time. "Thanks be to God, who in Christ always leads us in triumph, and through us spreads the fragrance of the knowledge of him everywhere" (2 Cor 2:15).

Appendix

"Evangelical Theology — Conservative and Contemporary" (This is the inaugural lecture delivered by Dr. Pinnock at the McMaster Divinity College in October, 1977 and published in the *Theological Bulletin* in May, 1978.)

Introduction

As a new professor at McMaster Divinity College I welcome this opportunity to share first with the alumni and friends assembled and now also with a wider audience my vision of what ought to characterize our theology and proclamation in a day of considerable doctrinal uncertainty, ferment and pluralism.[1] Because this is an essay in *theological method* the approach is broad and wide-ranging, but for the same reason it applies to almost every Christian concept and doctrine. After all, unanimity or discord in theological method is ultimately far more crucial than differences or agreements on particular beliefs simply because it affects every belief. My concern for theology, as the title suggests, is for it to be *evangelical*, *conservative*, and *contemporary*, and I shall begin by explaining what I mean.

1. *A Widespread Agreement*

The term 'evangelical' today is very imprecise and has been so historically. It has been employed since the Reformation in the 16th century to denote the Protestant as distinct from the Catholic effort to be faithful to the Gospel, and it has been used since then for less numerous groups within the Protestant coalition to indicate their efforts at a return to the authentic and original revelation. Although people differ on what they are pleased to call evangelical — for example, I am not altogether pleased to concede Schleiermacher's claim that *his* theology is evangelical[2] — nevertheless, it is a noble term indicating faithfulness to the Gospel, to an understanding of which this essay is also devoted.

In speaking of 'conservative' we have in mind an essential *fidelity* to the doctrinal structure of the biblical and Christian tradition. I doubt that a theology which lacked a conservative side would be entitled to the name Christian or evangelical. However much one may feel compelled to reword or revise the earlier understandings of the faith, there must surely be the intention to represent *this* structure of belief and not some other. By conservative I mean to indicate that there are limits to adaptation which we ought not to transgress because they are essential to the apostolic proclamation. We are expected to be faithful to the stewardship of the Gospel attested authoritatively in the Holy Scriptures, and maintain clear connections with the Word of God in our own theology and preaching.

By 'contemporary' I have in mind our proper *responsibility* to the contemporary hearers of the Gospel whereby we seek to communicate the message meaningfully to them and apply it creatively to the modern situation. Generally speaking, it is the failure to be contemporary which is the weakness of traditional orthodox theology and the failure to maintain clear continuity which is the weak spot in liberal theology. But I think there is a widespread desire on all sides to be *both* conservative and contemporary if possible; certainly it is my own fond wish.

In theological method, therefore, it is my conviction that our theology and preaching ought to be *bi-polar*: they should strive to be faithful to historical Christian beliefs taught in Scripture, and *at the same time* to be authentic and responsible to the contemporary hearers; or as Gilkey put it, to be "as authentically true to the Gospel as it is relevant to modernity."[4] Tillich puts it in terms of a correlation between the biblical message and the contemporary situation of modern man,[5] and on a popular level Francis A. Schaeffer tries to do this correlation too in his own way, to bring together biblical answers and existential questions.

At this level of generality I think there is considerable agreement about evangelical theology being conservative and contemporary, an important concensus that can serve as a basis for discussion on our differences. It is also a good measuring stick to use for our own theology and that of others, for asking, How do we measure up in terms of faithfulness to the Gospel, and responsibility to our hearers? *Evangelical* theology should be *conservative* and *contemporary*.

2. *Two Different Styles in Contemporary Theology*

When we move in closer, and pose questions to our bi-polar method, however, the degree of happy agreement begins to tarnish and diminish. What exactly is a faithful stewardship of Gospel and Creed? Do we mean, for example, the literal authority of the whole Canon of Scripture in its whole extent, or something less, a canon within the Canon? And as for our responsibility to the contemporary hearers we might ask with Thielicke, 'How modern should theology be?'[6] What degree of influence should the situation of modern man be permitted to exercise upon our theological reflections? Can modernity pose questions only, or answers also? Such questions as these force us to go deeper into the matter and begin to expose differences of opinion in theological method. They compel us to decide how we weigh the relative authority and status of the scriptural as opposed to the modernity pole, for example, and help to reveal *two distinctive approaches* to theology in our day.

Before proceeding I wish to acknowledge that there are other ways to 'cut the pie' than this, and that it makes a lot of difference to the outcome how the pie is cut. If, for example, we chose to arrange theological approaches according to their use or non-use of natural theology, the result would be very different from the typology discussed here, and it too would be important and worth discussing. In such an arrangement, to give an illustration, we would find Aquinas aligned with Hegel, and Calvin associated with Barth. Because they do not agree on the place to be accorded to natural reasoning in theology the 'orthodox' theologies would have to be shuffled amongst the two categories, and the same would happen to all the others as well.

Nevertheless, I think it is valuable and illuminating to identify and isolate the two basic approaches to theology in our time according to the weight they give to continuity and stewardship of the Gospel, and the role they allow to contemporary factors and beliefs. I wish to distinguish in this connection a *classical approach* from what I call the *liberal experiment*. In so doing I am not inventing the categories, although my preferred terminology may be novel,[7] but am following the lead taken by such theologians as Barth, Thielicke, Kenneth Hamilton, and others. I believe that this cleavage in contemporary theology is the most important distinction we can take note of, and, although the precise limits and exact membership in each group is fuzzy at the edges, I think we should be able to see the two basic families with some clarity.

A. Style One: The Classical Approach

Classical (conservative, orthodox) theology is characterized by a concentration upon fidelity and continuity with the historic Christian belief system set forth in Scripture and reproduced in creed and confession, with what C.S. Lewis called 'mere Christianity'. Prior to the rise of liberal theology in the 19th century, there was quite a consistency of approach to the normative priority of divine revelation in theology over the natural and uninspired thoughts of men and women, despite important differences in the interpretation of the sacred Writ. Certainly for the conservative Reformation the one and only foundation of Christian theology was believed to be the Word of God, uniquely and authoritatively attested in the Bible. Calvin wrote:

> By his Word God rendered faith unambiguous forever, a faith superior to all opinion .., no one can get even the slightest taste of right and sound doctrine unless he be a pupil of Scripture ... now daily oracles are not sent from heaven, for it pleased the Lord to hallow his truth to everlasting remembrance in the Scriptures alone. Hence the Scriptures obtain full authority among believers only when men regard them as having sprung from heaven, as if there the living words of God were heard.[8]

Similar sentiments could be produced from Luther, Menno, Wesley, and the great host of classical Christians who permitted no rival human opinion to compete in their minds with the written Word of God. Space will only permit, however, one other quotation from a Baptist source, the New Hampshire Confession, in an eloquent paragraph patterned on the Westminster Confession:

> We believe that the holy Bible was written by men divinely inspired, and is a perfect treasure of heavenly instruction; that it has God for its author, salvation for its end, and truth without any mixture of error for its matter; that it reveals the principles by which God will judge us; and therefore is, and shall remain to the end of the world, the true centre of Christian union, and

> the supreme standard by which all human conduct, creeds, and opinions should be tried.
>
> (Article 1)

Even Aquinas, although he believed that natural theology was a legitimate part of Christian theology, also considered the truth content of faith to come through divine revelation, not through natural reason.[9]

Classical Christians have always sought to exalt the truth of divine revelation, embodied in the Incarnation and attested in the Scriptures, far above the thoughts of mankind. They have considered the Bible to contain didactive thought models to guide their theology, models which were infallibly authoritative because they originated in God's witness to himself. For this reason they have shown themselves committed to an undiluted, we might say an undemythologized, biblical framework which enjoyed absolute cognitive authority over them. Let us hear from one classical, though contemporary theologian, B.B. Warfield:

> The confession of a supernatural God who may and does act in a supernatural mode, and who acting in a supernatural mode has wrought out for us a supernatural redemption, interpreted in a supernatural revelation, and applied by the supernatural operations of his Spirit — this confession constitutes the core of the Christian profession.[10]

Or, in terms of our subject, although the present situation is consulted, the contemporary *Geist* is not allowed to assume a normative position or become a normative principle affecting the revelational answers. Put in a nutshell, it is the contemporary questions that are revised in confrontation with the biblical text, not the text in correlation with the questions. The modernity pole is not permitted to compel any substantial revision of the original deposit of faith. Although St. Paul for example made every effort to adapt himself to the person or audience he was addressing, he was also prepared to go against and contradict the presuppositions of Jews and Greeks when they were incompatible with truth. He adamantly refused to compromise the divine mysteries of which he was a faithful steward. This is also the stance of classical Christianity. If the requirements of revelation are opposed to the current of contemporary thought, then Christians should be expected to swim *against the stream*, whether from within secularism, Marxism, capitalism, or humanism. We are not called to register, like a theological weathervane, which way the winds of old age are blowing, but rather to sail boldly into them.

At the same time, we must also register a criticism of classical theology for its frequent and relative neglect of the contemporary situation so that it has not always applied the Gospel in a fresh and creative manner. Of course it is wrong to let the world set the church's agenda, but it is also wrong to live in fear of modernity and in neglect of the contemporary situation of modern man as if God were no longer active in it and a sensitive response to contemporary modes of thought and feeling were no longer possible. After all, it is essential to express the Gospel *in context*, as preachers well know. Even the Scripture itself is an effort at contextualizing the Gospel in first century terms, requiring its readers to think carefully about its meaning and application today. Conservative Protestants today appear to be indifferent to contextual issues. It is *not* good enough to adopt a 16th century contextualizing of theology and simply to reprint and rehearse it in our generation. *That* is *not* faithfulness to the Gospel. We have not really been faithful to the truth until we have made it our own, and tried to express it with relevance in the new circumstances. Conservative Christianity needs to work much harder at formulating creative proposals of the biblical message for today. It is not enough to expose the unchristian assumptions of modernity unless we are prepared to do this task too. Somehow the classical doctrines have to be reappropriated in terms of modern experience, and this can be done without compromise with the help of the God who rules over every age and generation.

Modern conservatism has often become anti-cultural and world-denying in a bad sense. Just because we are alert to the sinful potentials in every phase of world culture does not require for us a moratorium on all appreciation of positive elements in modernity. The modern sense of outrage towards crimes against humanity, such as slavery, torture, and hunger, while it has some Christian roots itself, has called a neglectful church back to its own Bible and to the partial recovery of disturbing aspects of the Word conveniently forgotten for so long. Modern researches into social and psychological dimensions of human experience too are surely valuable tools, when used with discrimination, for getting at the intention of the scriptural message. There is no excuse for boycotting of these disciplines by so many conservative leaders today. Had we not gone through the Enlightenment with its critique of absolute social structures for example, we might never have recovered the biblical suggestions about democratic pluralism and feminine liberation. A good deal at least of the modern contempt of classical Christianity is due, not to the essence of its stand on Scripture, but to its non-essential narrowmindedness in regard to the gifts of common grace which the good Lord has freely given us.

In conclusion to this section, there is I believe a classical style of doing theology which is a distinct type of approach according to which divine revelation is viewed as a normative given, not to be adjusted or altered at the dictates of the world's beliefs. In the classical model the claims of modernity do not possess any inner-theological relevance. It may pose questions to us but cannot rival scriptural answers for us.

B. Style Two: The Liberal Experiment

With Friedrich Schleiermacher, the father of modern theology, a new approach to theology was initiated, and it can count within its number over the past century and a half some of the most creative Christian thinkers the church has ever known: Ritschl, Troeltsch, Harnack, Bultmann, Tillich and so forth. The liberal experiment in theology is *essentially* an effort at contextualization, and is *not* unconcerned, as some critics charge, about maintaining links with the Bible and classical beliefs. However, characteristic of the liberal experiment is a deep desire to make effective contact with the beliefs and experiences of modern man. It tends to concentrate upon the receiving "I" of the message (hence Thielicke calls it 'Cartesian' and Hamilton calls it 'hermeneutical'). It is very concerned with how belief is possible today, and is prepared to make use of an *outside criterion* as an aid in the understanding of the Gospel: for example, Heidegger's philosophy, or Husserl's phenomenology. Let us take some illustrations, being careful to avoid caricature or neglect of the great diversity within this approach.

Schleiermacher himself (d. 1834) took his departure from the religious dimension he detected in ordinary human experience, and sought to erect a dogmatic system based on a descriptive analysis of this sense of absolute dependence he saw in man. Religious experience became for him the criterion for assessing the teachings of the past and the means for reinterpreting the faith for modern man. To Karl Barth, Schleiermacher represented perfectly the liberal experiment which dwelt upon man's feelings rather than upon God's revealed Word. Out of this method emerged a theology of immanence and a Christology reckoned as an innate possibility of human nature. Whatever Schleiermacher's theology is, it is not classical Christianity.

August Sabatier, a French liberal theologian (d. 1901), affords another clear example of the liberal method in theology. In his book *The Religion of Authority and the Religion of the Spirit* published posthumously in 1904, Sabatier rejected classical Christian belief which was based on the authority of divine revelation in Scripture, and advocated in its place a religion of man's moral and spiritual experience, a version of the Quaker inner life.

Moving quickly ahead into the 20th century we pause to look at Bultmann's proposal for theology. When he made his initial call for believers to demythologize the New Testament (1941) he was not conscious of making a novel suggestion. He was perfectly aware, even if his readers were not, that the process of dismantling the biblical and orthodox framework of Christianity had been going on for a century already in the liberal experiment. To Bultmann, and in this he is simply a liberal, it was self-evident that a person could not sacrifice his modernity even for his faith. Indeed, it would be a treasonable act to force oneself to believe outdated notions. Instead, he proposed demythologizing these ideas — for example, the fall of man, the virgin birth, the atonement, the bodily resurrection, the second coming — and reinterpreting them in ways acceptable to the modern spirit, or more accurately compatible with the philosophical thinking of the early Heidegger.[11]

Schubert Ogden is an American interpreter and follower of Bultmann, as well as a leading light in the development of process theology, and because of a certain stridency peculiar to his writings Ogden expresses very lucidly the theological approach we are describing. Like his German mentor, Ogden finds the undemythologized New Testament message "unintelligible, incredible, and irrelevant" and contends that "no one could seriously maintain it." With Bultmann he is aware that demythologizing does not simply have to do with details in the text, but requires "the complete destruction of the traditional Christian conception of the 'history of salvation.'" And why is that? Simply because the demand to demythologize "arises with necessity from the situation of modern man and must be accepted without condition."[12] Granted, there are perhaps few who would express themselves in so forthright a manner and in a way so disturbing to classical Christians — we would not want to tar all liberals with Ogden's brush. Nevertheless, we have not found many of them condemning what he has to say, and we suspect is more of an exception in style than in content. From the conservative side, Ogden is an almost perfect example of 'apologetic' liberal theology which tailors the message of Scripture to suit the *Zeitgeist* because it does it so self-consciously and undeceptively.

On the popular market few books have sold more than *Honest to God* (1963), and it also represents the liberal experiment in theology admirably. Because the biblical understanding of God as creator outside the universe is repugnant to modern man, Robinson urges us to think of him as the ground of being, and because the supernaturalism of biblical and creedal Christology causes offense he suggests we think of Jesus in simply human terms, as the man for others. In order to achieve the desired relevance, we are asked to accept Jesus as a 'window into ultimate reality' rather than the divine son in whom the fulness of the godhead dwelled bodily. By these means the former bishop hopes to win inquirers to the Christian faith.

Earlier I referred to Paul Tillich as one who advocated the correlation of the biblical message with the situation of modern man. The way Tillich presents it, one would get the impression that the modern situation provides only questions and the Bible only answers in the correlation, but this is not so, and we need to correct that interpretation.[13] Deriving questions from the situation and answers from the Scriptures would in fact be the theological method of classical Christianity. In actual fact, in Tillich's theology the modern situation does most definitely provide answers as well as questions. Indeed his logos-philosophy, derived in large measure from German idealism, acts drastically upon the biblical message. There is in fact almost no biblical exegesis in the three volume work. Salvation becomes ontological reunion with the impersonal ground of being, instead of forgiveness through the atoning blood of Christ. Jesus becomes the historical symbol of an ontological principle, rather than the incarnation of the eternal Son of God. Kenneth Hamilton has gone so far as to say that "to see Tillich's system as a whole is to see that it is incompatible with the Christian gospel."[14] In a milder vein, it is no exaggeration to say that Tillich has created his 'system' out of materials at least partly present in philosophy not in Scripture, and does not acknowledge the authority of the Bible to critique and judge his thought.

Proceeding much more cautiously in these matters, Langdon Gilkey allows his theology to be heavily influenced by the secular philosophy of history. In his important recent book *Reaping the*

Whirlwind (1976), after revealing a sound grasp of the biblical and traditional understanding of God's providence, he finds it necessary on account of the critical standpoint to dismantle and reconstruct the historic Christian belief. He asks,

> How can the activity of God in social process be understood if history as a whole and political action within it are viewed at the deepest level naturalistically? This entire volume is devoted to an explication of and answer to this question.

His meaning becomes clear in two later statements:

> Our effort will be to reinterpret them (the classical concepts of providence) in the light of the modern historical consciousness which we share, and so to modify, if not dissolve entirely, these latter orthodox elements of the conception.
>
> We are seeking to avoid a 'supernaturalist' explanation of history and yet to find a valid and significant meaning for the conception of divine providence.[15]

It is surely plain that the modernity pole exercises for Gilkey hermeneutical authority over and above the scriptural text, and that he feels perfectly free to reinterpret the sacred text in accord with the modern self-understanding.

A particularly clear example of liberal theological method is supplied by the recent and highly praised book *Blessed Rage for Order* by David Tracy (1975). The modern theologian, he claims, has a double faith commitment, faith in the God of Jesus and faith in the modern experiment. Due to this double commitment, he is compelled to undertake a 'basic revision of traditional Christianity.'

The task the theologian has to perform involves providing an 'appropriate symbolic representation of the faith of secularity' and he claims that engaged in the task of basic revision are most of the leading American theologians today.[16]

It would be easy to go on giving illustrations of the liberal experiment until we had exhausted the prominent thinkers in this camp. We could dwell, for example, on the rather obvious case of process theology which quite openly relies on a philosophical source developed quite independently of Scripture and not subject to its critique, or on the Latin American theology of liberation which in at least some of its representatives (e.g. Gutierrez) insists on Marxist presuppositions in its explication of the Bible and of doctrine, not allowing them to be criticized by Scripture. But I think I have given enough illustrations in this section to establish that there is a non-classical approach to theology which I term the liberal experiment.

Here surely the weakness does not lie, as it does in much classical theology, in a relative neglect of the contemporary situation, but rather on the other side of the equation, in a certain loss of continuity with Scripture and tradition. In all of these cases, to a lesser or greater degree, the modern spirit is exalted alongside God's Word in the form of a *rival commitment*. A theology of relevance is pursued with such zeal that even central affirmations of Scripture are allowed to be lost in order to gain a hearing. The use of an outside criterion by which to understand the kerygma appears to allow the Gospel itself to come under alien control. Instead of Scripture being the norm, theology is governed by the 19th or 20th century cultural ego instead.[17]

Not wishing to be unfair, let us freely admit that the liberal experiment was right in its desire to be relevant and authentic, and was not usually motivated by the desire to jettison the basic doctrines of Christianity, although it often happened. Nevertheless, it represents a distinct theological style or type according to which Scripture is criticized and its contents demythologized on the strength of what modern man believes. Modernity, as well as Scripture, is allowed to give answers to theology — modern man gives revelation to himself. Obviously there is a deep disagreement about theological method and sources which the initial agreement we noted earlier masked. Unlike classical theology which seeks to place itself under the Word, the liberal experiment is determined to place modernity on a par and often even above the Scripture.

3. *Evangelical Theology — Conservative and Contemporary*

What we are seeking is a theology which maintains a proper *balance of newness and oldness*, which does justice both to the authoritative Scriptures, and to the needs of the contemporary hearers. After all, the Christian message, as John said, is old and getting older, and yet, paradoxically, is ever new (1 Jn 2:7). My vision is for a theology which is *faithful* to what God has said, and *responsible* to the people who hear it. Let us consider how this balance can be achieved and maintained.

First, consider the conservative side of theology, the issue of fidelity and continuity with the faith once delivered. As in classical theology, I believe we all ought to stand underneath God's defining revelation, within the framework of covenantal truth deposited in Scripture. After all, we are not 'free-thinkers' but those who confess the lordship of Jesus and who are sent out under his authority with his message. Divinely inspired Scripture is, and has always been, the limiting factor, the objective input, the creative and life-giving source for theology. There are many New Testament texts to guide us here. The central theme of *2 Timothy*, for example, is one of guarding and continuing in the Gospel (1:13-14, 3:14). To that end Paul urges Timothy to treat the message with utmost respect, and to ensure that it is passed down to the next generation intact (2:1-2, 4:1-5). Its terms are authoritatively set forth in the God-breathed Scriptures, and in the apostle's own writings and teachings (3:14-17). Timothy needs to be watchful because there is a real danger that the sacred truth deposit will be manipulated and distorted (3:1-9). It is as if Paul were speaking directly to the liberal experiment, and issuing a note of extreme caution.

Another relevant image of Paul's which applies here is that of a stewardship of the Gospel. He regards himself as a faithful steward of the mysteries of God (1 Cor 4:1-2). As such, he will not consider tampering in any way with the message (2 Cor 4:2). The trustee or steward does not add or subtract from the lord's commission, but faithfully preserves and presents it — it is his authority, as well as his glory. Paul proclaimed the Gospel boldly as he did because he believed it to be founded upon what God had said. There are many texts in the New Testament which command us to stand firm in the truth, to pay close attention to what we have heard, to contend for the faith once delivered to the saints (2 Thess 2:15 Gal 1:8-9 Heb 2:1 Jude 3). We live in a generation which is suspicious of the old and confident in the new. The oldness of the faith is a stumbling block to many people, but it cannot be otherwise. What God has said in the Gospel and in the Scripture is final and definitive. We have a solemn duty to preach it and pass it along.

We need to regain our convictions about an essentially *unchanging* Gospel in an essentially changing world. Mascall has put it eloquently,

> The hard core of Christian truth is the same for one age and place as for another. Its claim is not to be new, but to be permanent; and, while it has the most wonderful power to address men and women where they stand, it must also sometimes point out to them that they are

standing in the wrong place or that the place where they are standing is not where they think it is.

In saying that people must be told when they are standing in the wrong place, Mascall opens up for us the great objection to the liberal experiment, its willingness to purchase contemporaneity at the high price of critiquing Scripture and canonizing uninspired opinion and its reluctance to place contemporary mythologies under the judgement of the Word of God. It is not Christian thought which needs to be brought into line with modern thought, but modern man who needs to be intellectually and spiritually converted to the Gospel message.

The most objectionable feature of the liberal experiment then is the way in which it places human wisdom on a par with the Word of God. What possible justification could there be, in view of the New Testament teaching about wisdom in the old age outside of Christ, for using modern man's understanding of reality as a critical instrument for judging Scripture (1 Cor. 1:18-31 3:18-23)? By all means let us seek to be relevant — but not at any price. The function of God's Word is to shatter man's twisted illusions, not to sanctify them. To modernize, enculturate, or secularize the Gospel is a treasonable act, on a par with Israel's repeated efforts to join Baal and Yahweh worship, and results from a failure to stand up for the truth in a threatening or seductive environment.

Paul warns us to beware of 'philosophy', that is, to guard against being captured by a man-made system of religious speculations which would rival the truth of the Gospel. Today there are themes in culture which call for vigilance and resistance from Christian people. While seeking to respond creatively to our time, we must exert *counter-pressures* upon our environment, and avoid capitulating to error. We have a responsibility to expose *non*christian assumptions in the dominant culture. Although this is sometimes done from within the liberal experiment, it is not done consistently or thoroughly, humanism and secularism are seldom challenged and refuted at basic levels.[19] What excuse can be offered for the persistent tendency to chip away at biblical supernaturalism instead of calling into question modern anti-supernaturalism? Why is Bultmann so much admired when he states explicitly that what motivates his proposal to demythologize is his pseudo-scientific conviction of a closed continuum of cause and effect which renders God's mighty acts impossible?[20] And why do we give so much attention to such biblical criticism as takes its departure from this kind of secularism? Surely James D. Smart is correct in blaming the tragic silence of the Bible in the modern church with all its disastrous effects on criticism of this kind.[21] No wonder modern preachers schooled in a subchristian approach to the biblical documents find themselves robbed of definite convictions and a clear, forceful message. Conversely, it is no accident or secret that the churches which are growing in North America are those in which solid biblical convictions are maintained and proclaimed with no uncertain sound.[22] We are called to be faithful to the Gospel.

Second, consider the contemporary side of theology, the issue of responsibility and authenticity. Earlier we indicted conservative theology for its relative neglect of the contemporary situation in doing its work, for slighting the task of contextualizing the Gospel. It would be a sad picture if Scripture were seen to be a limit and restriction, without any room left for freedom and creativity. Indeed there is a liberating factor, the reality of the living God who leads and guides his people who are in *context*. God makes it a liberating Word for us as he unveils its sense and enables them to be *faithful-in* context. We have hope in the Spirit of God who abides with the church, and leads us deeper into all truth. Scripture is normative, but needs always to be read afresh and applied in new ways. Because it is God's word, it is new in each situation, and fresh to every person desiring to be renewed by it. In Wesley, and Carey, and Booth we see Christian leaders convinced of the permanent relevance and power of the Gospel, refusing to be shackled by churchly traditions, and willing to break out in new patterns, while remaining faithful and true to the scriptural revelation. There is no contradiction between faithfulness to God's written word, and a daring openness to look for creative ways to express the living Christ in our generation. In C.S. Lewis, a man whose influence appears to be still growing, we sense one who was able to create a highly original statement of wholly unoriginal doctrine. Faithfulness and creativity — it can be done!

We are certainly not advocating static conservatism. Fidelity does not consist in simply repeating old formulae drafted in an earlier time. It includes the creative thinking required to make the old message fresh and new. New expressions are needed just to maintain the old truths, giving them relevance in the new circumstances. Even though we insist on keeping to the guidelines laid down in Scripture, there is also ample room for creativity in our proposal of the

Christian message for our day. In Christology, for example, we must of course preserve the great truth of the incarnation over against efforts to demythologize it,[21] but it is also possible to be very sensitive to the desire of our generation to be in touch with his real humanness and to do justice to Jesus' distinctiveness as a man. In the doctrine of God, we must preserve the truth of God as creator, ruler, and Lord over all against the immanence philosophies of our day, and yet at the same time there is no reason why we should not emphasize the dynamism of the biblical portrait of God rather than the static approach in classical theism not only because of its truth but because of its relevance to our generation. In the doctrine of Scripture, we must certainly uphold the classical confidence, documented in the Bible itself, in God speaking authoritatively in the canonical text, but we can also make a greater effort to be honest and observant in regard to the human side of Scripture as well which is a more recent concern in biblical studies. In short, I see a kind of theological synthesis possible in which the Bible remains normative, but in which it is read afresh for the illumination of the Spirit who makes the letter of Scripture live for us.

Conclusion

What I long to see is an *evangelical* theology which is *conservative* in its guarding of the Gospel and *contemporary* in the task of its application to our generation in the power of the Spirit. It would be a theology which kept a proper balance of oldness and newness, marked by an ability to maintain the classical truth of the Gospel and communicate it without compromise in the new situation in fresh and creative ways. It is a better dialectic of Word and Spirit that we are seeking, confidence in the Word from *outside* the human situation, and reliance on the Spirit to make it fresh and new.

The essay would be incomplete if we did not at this point say a little more about the Spirit's work. After all, modern theology is much exercised about how faith is possible, and yet the Spirit's great specialty is in creating faith and communication. It is he who gives us access to the deep things of God (1 Cor 2:11). Calvin said:

> God sent down his Spirit by whose power he dispensed the word to complete his work by the efficacious confirmation of the Word. (Bk. 2, ch. 9)

If we are concerned to show how relevant the Gospel is, perhaps what we need to attend to is not demythologizing but rather renewal in the Spirit whose power it is to take the undiluted Word of God and use it to reach and to save sinners. I am convinced therefore that the bi-polar method in theology cannot succeed in a community which lacks vital spirituality. As Ramm puts it,

> The evangelical believes that the real touchstone of a theology is its spiritual power not necessarily its intellectual shrewdness or sophistication or learning.[24]

Seminary professors like myself prefer to think that the most creative proposals for a balanced theology will come from the academic community. But it may not be so. The criteria for good judgement in theology are not handed over with the doctoral diploma. In the realm of the Spirit the critical factor is spiritual power not human intelligence. We are often attracted by the novel theology which comes up with a brilliant fusion between the Bible and something contemporary. But this is not what God is after. He desires us to be faithful stewards of his Word, who do not seek glory in this age, and do not value what man thinks above what God has said, but open ourselves to his Spirit, walk by faith and not by sight, and proclaim the Gospel with fearlessness and undiminished power.

Notes

Introduction

1. J. Gresham Machen did not exaggerate when he wrote: "The great redemptive religion known as Christianity is battling against a totally diverse type of religious belief, which is only the more destructive of the Christian faith because it makes use of traditional Christian terminology." *Christianity and Liberalism* (Grand Rapids: Eerdmans, 1923 reprint).
2. Donald Bloesch describes the kind of evangelical theology which I also gladly confess. *The Future of Evangelical Christianity, a Call for Unity Amid Diversity* (Garden City, NY: Doubleday, 1983).
3. I want to acknowledge my deep appreciation for two recent books which have the same kind of urgency and direction as my own. Francis A. Schaeffer, *The Great Evangelical Disaster* (Westchester, Crossway Books, 1984) and Franky Schaeffer, *Bad News for Modern Man* (Westchester, Crossway Books, 1984). I realize afresh how profoundly the L'Abri themes have affected me ever since I was a worker there in 1966 and a student there in years before that.

Chapter One

1. John R. W. Stott, one of the truly great evangelicals of the twentieth century, emphasizes this point about guarding the gospel in several of his books: *The Preacher's Portrait* (London: The Tyndale Press, 1961), *Christ the Controversialist* (London: The Tyndale Press, 1970), *Guard the Gospel, The Message of 2 Timothy* (London: Inter-Varsity Press, 1973).
2. I recommend highly the discussion of the four marks of the church including apostolicity in Hans Küng, *The Church* (New York: Sheed and Ward, 1967) pp. 263-359.
3. Michael Novak takes his stand in *Confessions of a Catholic* (San Francisco: Harper & Row, 1983). Edward Farley glumly notes the same truth while deploring it: *Ecclesial Reflection, An Anatomy of Theological Method* (Philadelphia: Fortress Press, 1982).

4. Obviously I am not alone in feeling this way but belong to a large and growing number of theologians who are recovering their biblical roots. See, for example, Thomas C. Oden, *Agenda for Theology, Recovering Christian Roots* (San Francisco: Harper & Row, 1979).
5. I appreciate Gilkey's clarity in describing what has happened, though I deplore his approving of it. *Naming the Whirlwind, The Renewal of God-Language* (New York: Bobbs-Merrill, 1969) p. 76-77.
6. In case you think I am exaggerating, and want to check it out for yourself, see a volume which makes no bones about the 'revision' (their word for betrayal): *Christian Theology, An Introduction to its Traditions and Tasks*, edited by Peter C. Hodgson and Robert H. King (Philadelphia: Fortress Press, 1982).
7. As I write these words, let me admit that I am aware of the severe tension we all experience in the modern world between historical and ahistorical modes of thinking, and of its implications for a message which claims 'the Word became flesh' and 'the Bible is both divine and human.' Grant Wacker has been pointing out this tension in the work of the great conservative A. H. Strong In addition to several essays, see his yet unpublished manuscript *Augustus H. Strong and the Dilemma of Historical Consciousness*.
8. This whole subject has been wonderfully treated by Bruce A. Demarest, *General Revelation, Historical Views and Contemporary Issues* (Grand Rapids: Zondervan, 1982).
9. For a learned discussion of the shift in views on the function of the Bible as canon, see David H. Kelsey, *The Uses of Scripture in Recent Theology* (Philadelphia: Fortress Press, 1975).
10. Some evangelicals like Dr Schaeffer feel very strongly that inerrancy is the term we must use at this point of history to protect and preserve the historic conviction about Scripture. I see his point and agree about the importance of the conviction itself. But the term has certain disadvantages which to me make it less than essential. See Pinnock, *The Scripture Principle* (San Francisco: Harper & Row, 1984).
11. The best conservative book on the doctrine of God may be Jack Cottrell, *What the Bible Says About God the Creator* (Joplin, Missouri: College Press, 1983). I should also mention the Carl F.H. Henry *magnum opus* whose two final volumes are given over to the doctrine of God as well. *God, Revelation and Authority*, volumes five and six (Waco, Texas: Word Inc., 1982 and 1983).
12. Langdon Gilkey, *Message and Existence, An Introduction to Christian Theology* (New York: The Seabury Press, 1979), chapter 7. This whole book shaped as it is upon the doctrine of the Trinity is a deception since no trinity is affirmed in the proper sense of the term.
13. Donald Bloesch, *Essentials of Evangelical Theology* (San Francisco: Harper & Row, 1978) ch 6. For a stirring defense of the incarnation and salvation through Christ, see H.P. Owen, *Christian Theism, A*

Study in Its Basic Principles (Edinburgh: T. & T. Clark, 1984), ch. 3 and 6.

14. For modern developments on the doctrine of atonement, see Fisher Humphreys, *The Death of Christ* (Nashville: Broadman Press, 1978).
15. See the important recent book by Colin Brown, *Miracles and the Critical Mind* (Grand Rapids: Eerdmans, 1984).
16. Maurice Wiles called his book *Remaking* but knows the proper term is 'Unmaking': *The Remaking of Christian Doctrine* (Philadelphia: The Westminster Press, 1978), p. 103.
17. I have not read a clearer analysis of this sort of thing than James Hitchcock, *What Is Secular Humanism?* (Ann Arbor: Servant Books, 1982) ch 8.
18. Most surveys of contemporary theology seem to ignore this issue, though in reality they simply decide it in the liberal mode and proceed from there. See Deane W. Ferm, *Contemporary American Theologies, A Critical Survey* (New York: The Seabury Press, 1981).
19. My efforts to defend the faith can be found in two modest books: *Set Forth Your Case* (Craig Press, 1967) and *Reason Enough* (Downers Grove: Inter Varsity Press, 1980). Francis Schaeffer was worried about the evangelical slide into what he called a 'new neo-orthodoxy' in which Christians would back away from strong truth claims regarding the gospel and content themselves with existential experiences. I am sympathetic with this concern too. *The Great Evangelical Disaster*, pp. 49-65.

Chapter Two

1. The best book on the theology of revival and our prospects of seeing it in our time is Richard F. Lovelace, *Dynamics of Spiritual Life, an Evangelical Theology of Renewal* (Downers Grove: Inter Varsity Press, 1979).
2. In liberal systematic theologies, the Spirit turns out to represent the omnipresence of God and not the release of eschatological power: for example, Gordon D. Kaufman, *Systematic Theology, A Historicist Perspective* (New York: Charles Scribner's Sons, 1968) ch. 15-16 or L. Harold DeWolf, *A Theology of the Living Church* (New York: Harper & Row, 1953) ch 32.
3. George T. Montague, *The Holy Spirit, Growth of a Biblical Tradition* (New York: Paulist Press, 1976).
4. Rodman Williams, *The Era of the Spirit* (Plainfield, NJ: Logos International, 1971) and *The Pentecostal Reality* (Plainfield, NJ: Logos International, 1972) ch 3.
5. This point is best brought out by David Watson, *I Believe in Evangelism* (Grand Rapids: Eerdmans, 1976).
6. J.I. Packer, "Steps to the Renewal of Christian People", in *Summons to*

Faith and Renewal, Christian Renewal in a Post-Christian World, edited by Peter S. Williamson and Kevin Perrotta (Ann Arbor: Servant Books, 1983) pp. 107-127.
7. George Mallone deals with all the arguments for cessation in *Those Controversial Gifts* which he edited (Downers Grove: Inter Varsity Press, 1983) ch 1.
8. You can read Cassidy's testimony in his book *Bursting the Wineskins* (Wheaton: Harold Shaw, 1983).
9. George T. Montague, *Riding the Wind, Learning the Ways of the Spirit* (Ann Arbor: Word of Life, 1974) p. 17.
10. Read Charles Hummel's testimony and wise analysis of what has been happening: *Fire in the Fireplace, Contemporary Charismatic Renewal* (Downers Grove: Inter Varsity Press, 1978).

Chapter Three

1. For a responsible survey of the prophetic dimension, see R.E.O. White, *Biblical Ethics* (Exeter: Paternoster Press, 1979). A second volume has appeared: *Christian Ethics* (Atlanta: John Knox Press, 1981).
2. I have a growing appreciation for what has been called postmillennial eschatology as a practical policy to guide Christian action and morale. See R. J. Rushdoony, *God's Plan for Victory, The Meaning of Post Millennialism* (Fairfax, Virginia: Thoburn Press, 1980).
3. The reader is referred to some good treatments of these adverse social changes: Peter Williamson and Kevin Perrotta, editors, *Christianity Confronts Modernity* (Ann Arbor: Servant Books, 1981) and *Summons to Faith and Renewal* (Ann Arbor: Servant Books, 1983).
4. See David O. Moberg, *The Great Reversal, Evangelism Versus Social Concern* (New York: Lippincott, 1972). A more recent look at the problem is Dennis P. Hollinger, *Individualism and Social Ethics, An Evangelical Syncretism* (Lanham, Md.: University Press of America, 1983).
5. Donald Bloesch discusses the ideological temptation in *The Future of Evangelical Theology*, pp. 67-79.
6. Systematic studies of what *Sojourners* has been communicating are beginning to appear. The first one is worth reading even though it seems to have been prepared in haste: Joan Harris, *The Sojourners File* (Washington: New Century Foundation Press, 1983).
7. See Ernest W. Lefever, *Amsterdam to Nairobi, The World Council of Churches and the Third World* (Washington: Ethics and Public Policy Center, 1979).
8. See Rael and Erich Isaac, "Sanctifying Revolution", in their important book *Coercive Utopians* (Chicago: Henry Regnery, 1983).

9. I agree entirely with the direction of thought in Michael Novak, *The Spirit of Democratic Capitalism* (New York: Simon & Schuster, 1982). Novak made a similar shift in his thought from left-wing utopianism to democratic realism that I too have experienced.
10. Paul Hollander, *Political Pilgrims, Travels of Western Intellectuals to the Soviet Union, China, and Cuba 1928-1978* (New York: Oxford University Press, 1981).
11. Jean-Francois Revel, *The Totalitarian Temptation* (Garden City, NY: Doubleday & Co Inc, 1977).
12. The gruesome story is told at length by Paul Johnson, *A History of the Modern World, From 1917 to the 1980's* (London: Weidenfeld and Nicolson, 1983). The book is entitled *Modern Times* in the United States.
13. This is the burden of P.T. Bauer among others. See his most recent titles: *Equality, The Third World and Economic Delusion* (London: Weidenfeld and Nicolson, 1981) and *Reality and Rhetoric, Studies in the Economics of Development* (London: Weidenfeld and Nicolson, 1984).
14. Milton and Rose Friedman, *Free to Choose, A Personal Statement* (New York: Harcourt Brace Jovanovich, 1980).
15. Lord Peter Bauer's famous essay "Western Guilt and Third World Poverty" is must reading: *Equality, the Third World and Economic Delusion*, ch. 4.
16. The economic claims made in the name of liberation theology are truly astonishing in their ability to deceive. See *Liberation Theology*, Ronald H. Nash, editor (Milford, Michigan: Mott Media, 1984); Michael Novak, editor, *Liberation South, Liberation North* (Washington: American Enterprise Institute, 1981); Michael Novak, *The Spirit of Democratic Capitalism*, ch 16-18.
17. "Ethical Reflections on the Economic Crisis" from the social affairs commission of the Canadian Conference of Catholic Bishops, January, 1983. For a commentary and discussion which enthusiastically supports these recommendations, see Gregory Baum and Duncan Cameron, *Ethics and Economics, Canada's Catholic Bishops on the Economic Crisis* (Toronto: James Lorimer, 1984).
18. For the text of the bishops reflections and a series of rather devastating critiques by James Finn, Richard J. Neuhaus, Paul Heynes, Thomas Langan, and some others: *This World* 5 (1983) pp. 122-145.
19. For a searching critique of what the bishops said, see Walter Block, *On Economics and the Canadian Bishops* (Vancouver: The Fraser Institute, 1983).
20. "I know of no example in time or place of a society that has been marked by a large measure of political freedom, and that has not also used something comparable to a free market to organize the bulk of

economic activity." Milton Friedman, *Capitalism and Freedom* (Chicago: University of Chicago Press, 1962) p. 9.

21. The dismal record of human rights violation in the USSR and every other communist regime is well known. See John W. Montgomery, "The Marxist Approach to Human Rights: Analysis and Critique", *The Simon Greenleaf Law Review* 3 (1983-84) pp. 3-202.
22. Franky Schaeffer is especially vehement in his anger over the butchery of abortion. What kind of moral discernment is it which is blind to this evil? Schaeffer, *Bad News to Modern Man*, ch. 1.
23. For a more sympathetic analysis, see a book appropriately entitled *The Welfare State in Crisis* by Ramesh Mishra (Brighton, Sussex: Wheatsheaf Books, 1984).
24. Canada's politics of appeasement put forward under the guise of seeking peace in a divided world might as well be orchestrated by the Kremlin. A great deal of contemporary peace-talking is not peacemaking and is likely to lead to capitulation or to war itself. See *Who Is For Peace?* by Francis Schaeffer, Vladimir Bukovsky, and James Hitchcock (Nashville: Thomas Nelson, 1983).

Conclusion

1. Gerald Bray draws this conclusion from a fine study of early Christian doctrine: *Creeds, Councils and Christ* (Downers Grove, Illinois: Inter Varsity Press, 1984).

Appendix "Evangelical Theology — Conservative and Contemporary"

1. D. Tracy, *Blessed Rage for Order* (New York: Seabury Press, 1975), ch. 1.
2. F. Schleiermacher, *The Christian Faith* (ET, T. & T. Clark, 1928, Fortress Press, 1976), p. vii.
3. A. Dulles, *The Resilient Church, The Necessity and Limits of Adaptation* (New York: Doubleday, 1977).
4. L. Gilkey, *Catholicism Confronts Modernity* (New York: Seabury Press, 1976), p. 9.
5. Later on in this essay I will register my belief that Tillich's practice of correlation is much less acceptable than his theory.
6. H. Thielicke, *How Modern Should Theology Be?* (Philadelphia: Fortress, 1969).
7. Thielicke likes to call the liberal experiment 'Cartesian' because of its preoccupation with the believing subject, and Hamilton labels it simply 'earth-bound' in *Revolt Against Heaven* (Grand Rapids: Eerdmans, 1965). cf. Thielicke, *The Evangelical Faith* (Grand Rapids: Eerdmans, 1974), I part 1.

8. J. Calvin, *Institutes of the Christian Religion*, Book I, Ch. 6-7.
9. E. Gilson, *The Christian Philosophy of Saint Thomas Aquinas* (New York: Random House, 1956), p. 10.
10. B. Warfield, *Biblical and Theological Studies* (Philadelphia: Presbyterian and Reformed Publishing Company, 1952), p. 21.
11. cf. R. Bultmann, *Jesus Christ and Mythology* (London: SCM, 1960), *Kergyma and Myth* (New York: Harper & Row, 1961).
12. S. Ogden, *Christ Without Myth* (New York: Harper & Row, 1961), pp. 24, 37, 127.
13. P. Tillich, *Systematic Theology* (Chicago: University of Chicago Press, 1961), pp. 59-66.
14. K. Hamilton, *The System and the Gospel* (London: SCM, 1963), p. 227.
15. L. Gilkey, *Reaping the Whirlwind* (New York: Seabury Press, 1976), pp. 199, 240, 247.
16. D. Tracy, *Blessed Rage for Order* (New York: Seabury Press, 1975). p. 4.
17. This concern has been recently expressed by the *Hartford Declaration* issued in January, 1975.
18. E. L. Mascall, *The Christian Universe* (London: Darton, Longman and Todd, 1966), p. 13.
19. A. Dulles, *The Resilient Church, The Necessity and Limits of Adaptation* (New York: Doubleday, 1977) ch. 4.
20. R. Bultmann, *Existence and Faith* (London: Fontana, 1964), p. 345.
21. J.D. Smart, *The Strange Silence of the Bible in the Church* (Philadelphia: Westminster, 1970), pp. 9-10.
22. D. Kelly, *Why the Conservative Churches are Growing* (New York: Harper & Row, 1972).
23. e.g. J. Hick, editor, *The Myth of God Incarnate* (London: SCM, 1977).
24. B. Ramm, *The Evangelical Heritage* (Waco: Word Inc., 1973), p. 146.